ZEN AND THE ART OF

Street Fighting

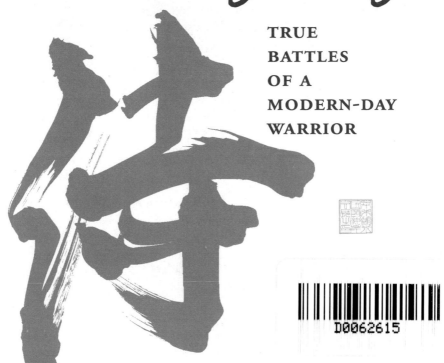

**TRUE
BATTLES
OF A
MODERN-DAY
WARRIOR**

JACK SABAT

Frog, Ltd.
Berkeley, California

Zen and the Art of Street Fighting: True Battles of a Modern-Day Warrior

Copyright © 1996 by Jack M. Sabat. All rights reserved. No portion of this book, except for brief review, may be reproduced, stored in a retrieval system, or transmitted in any form—electronic, mechanical, photocopying, or recording—without prior written permission of the publisher. For information, contact Frog, Ltd. c/o North Atlantic Books. Printed in the United States of America.

Published by Frog, Ltd.

Frog, Ltd. books are distributed by
North Atlantic Books
P.O. Box 12327
Berkeley, California 94712

Distributed to the book trade by Publishers Group West

Cover calligraphy and photo credit by Naoki Hongo
Cover and book design by Paula Morrison

Library of Congress Cataloging-in-Publication data
Sabat, Jack M., 1946–
    Zen and the art of street fighting : true battles of a modern-day warrior / Jack M. Sabat.
        p.   cm.
    ISBN 1-883319-45-5
    1. Sabat, Jack M., 1946–   .   2. Martial artists—Biography
I. Title.
GV1113.S24A3   1996
791.43'028'092—dc20
[B]   96-23671
                                                                    CIP

1   2   3   4   5   6   7   8   9   /   00   99   98   97   96

ZEN AND THE ART OF

Street Fighting

ACKNOWLEDGMENTS

For my Sensei who showed me the Way
and to those whose love for real *Budo* prevails—

My appreciation to:

My wife, who stood by me when doubt challenged the Journey.

My student and friend, Roy Ogden, who made things ring true.

To the forces that guide my Spirit.

CONTENTS

FOREWORD

My intention is to make you think: to make you step outside the comfort zone where you are familiar and safe. It is there where your search for *satori* (enlightenment)—"the pinnacle of peace"—which will leave you drifting in and out of calm and violent seas. It is on this journey where you must learn to seek the highest level of the Zen mind—*Sei Chuu Do*—potential movement within stillness.

The Japanese martial arts are a means to an end. Through these arts, the practitioner becomes like a bamboo shoot, surviving through great resiliency. As the roots of the bamboo are deep and strong, the bamboo can resist the destructive forces of nature. Just before the bowed bamboo snaps under the weight of the accumulated winter snow, it twists and shifts, springing upright and causing the snow to the fall to the earth. This is the essence of *Budo*—that which allows one to change and adapt to life's different challenges. The amount of change causes a like amount of growth, and so in life one becomes great if one becomes adaptable.

This book reveals a part of my awakening, and one man's battles against the predictable forces of man and the unpredictable force of nature. As *Budo* has become diluted in modern times, it is my true hope that those *Budoka* of the old days still live and reflect the essence of *Budo,* to keep it alive in a few small corners of our world. Hopefully, this book will cast but a glimmer of light on the path to enlightenment of the self and awaken the reader to the real meaning of practice.

These stories are true. They tell of trials and tribulations. I have joined them with ancient and modern training methods which have been tested on the battlefield. I learned these methods from my Sensei. I still use them today. The study of *Budo samurai* battles and the forces of nature help to put my own martial arts ordeals in perspective.

They help to explain what valor has meant to me. Change is the law of nature and one must never forget that in the face of danger, the resiliency one achieves through *Budo,* like that of the bamboo shoot, depends not only on honor, loyalty, and truth, but on the depth of one's roots and the will to sustain ancient and honorable traditions.

It is my greatest hope that you will use this battle book as a means to seek higher learning and a catalyst to charge your spirit and train harder. Cast safety aside, make risk your target, and become triumphant. Strive for the honorable goal of *really living,* as each one of us is destined to die some day. Make the practice of *Budo* constant and forever changing like a river; seek out the universal light. Train in the *Budo* arts—a beautiful violence to find unshakable peace.

This is my story.

Jack Sabat

ZEN AND THE ART OF

Street Fighting

Ki—Spirit

CHAPTER ONE

The Steel Dojo

"Hajime!" Sensei commanded. My opponent launched a furious attack. I stepped back and off to the side. In an explosive blur of kicks—front kicks, side kicks, hooking Chinese-style kicks—my opponent continued to advance as if expecting to force his victory. I was constantly moving, sliding, and slipping the assault, hoping that he would blow out like a spent candle. I sensed his approaching exhaustion. Suddenly and defiantly, I stood my ground.

The grey steel hull of the massive aircraft carrier cut through the dark waters with an eerie silence.

It was an unsettling feeling and it was hidden deep within me. I knew life held a great mission for me in some future time and place. I had always played the role of leader and found myself assisting others in distress. I found the proper means to seek a higher understanding of life and fulfill my destiny one muggy day off the coast of Viet Nam. How a rock-and-roll high school kid in the 1960s found his destiny during a time of war is the first chapter in my modern-day martial arts saga. Martial arts marked the beginning of my lifelong mission in the midst of heavy battle in the skies over Viet Nam, the jewel of Southeast Asia.

At that time, my home was miles away on the other side of the world and the calm seemed everlasting while at sea off the Asian continent. I spent a year being moved around in the military until I landed on a ship for what seemed like an eternal tour of duty. I dug in and remained on the *USS Kittyhawk*, a CVA-63 aircraft carrier, my new home. The carrier is about the size of two football fields with enough ordnance to destroy a small city. Relaxation was found in the oddest places: from watching poisonous sea snakes sunning themselves belly-up in the water to observing the Marines on the fantail peppering the drifting garbage with powerful M-16 rounds. The muzzle flashes lit up the night sky like sparks from a flint. Time passed slowly and you had to seek out some type of escape lest you go crazy in the middle of nowhere.

After a stay of sixty days at sea off the coast of Viet Nam, tempers became short and nerves were easily shattered. The tension seemed to rise as we moved closer to land. We envisioned the Philippines and the irresistible night life of Olongapo, the city on Subic Bay near the massive military installation there. As the aircraft carrier rounded the bend at the peninsula, we seemed to enter the bay in slow motion. I stood on the forward catwalk observing the scenery, feeling the emotion only sailors understand when they see land again after a long time at sea. I was looking forward to some badly needed R & R—rest and relaxation. Some of my shipmates were hanging out discussing their plans for the two-week stay in port. It was the usual talk of where they would go, what girl they hoped to see, or, most often, how much beer they planned to drink.

The war seemed far away as I watched palm trees swaying in the wind along the sun-bleached shore. The locals in the water appeared to welcome not only our arrival, but the smell of American money and the many ways they had devised to carefully relieve us of it. The ship slowly steamed past Grande Island, a place accessible only by boat where service personnel could raise hell or relax in relative safety. Grande Island was unlike Olongapo, where trouble lurked at every corner. Cool tropical surf pounded the beach, changing colors with each wave like an artist's canvas. Ocean water danced in compliance with nature as sea gulls accompanied our ship on its slow approach to the harbor. In the distance I could observe the shore and docking personnel gathering for our arrival. The ocean tugs slowly pushed us into position to secure the ship in its proper berth. This orchestration continued day in and day out, as the giant war machine turned and ground its way forward during the Viet Nam crisis.

I wondered how many sailors and Marines would get to go home after the war. My mind drifted as the intense sunlight bathed my face. The flight deck was quiet behind me. Why was I here? I constantly asked myself this question, wishing somehow to find the answer. It was a year earlier that I asked myself that same question in boot camp before I received my transfer orders to the *USS Kittyhawk*. I continued my search for the answer after my arrival on board the carrier.

At that time, the *Kittyhawk* was one of the largest aircraft carriers in the world. She was a fighting fortress with the charm of a metropolitan universal city. It was easy to get lost among the maze of winding passageways, steel doors, and steel catwalks.

Everywhere the signs of warfare and munitions and stores of a warring faction were present. Danger lurked at every turn because of rows and stacks of bombs you had to step across. It was a perilous journey just to walk to dinner amidst the aircraft, dodging a missile waiting on the deck or hanging from the belly of a fighter. Continually present were the armed Marines who guarded over the delicate matters and sensitive tasks carried out by the officers on board.

The hangar bay was the working heart of the carrier. There, the countless missiles and bombs were loaded by young airmen before flight operations sent them skyward to their designated targets. Only time and fate would prove their mission to be a success or a failure.

I had come from a middle-class neighborhood in the heart of the Midwest and now found myself engaged in a war no one wanted. Yet no one would talk of a "foolish" war in the presence of any gung-ho heroes. It was during this turbulent time that I wondered where my destiny would take me. I questioned the sense of committing to a four-year tour of duty. Back home during the 1960s, the would-be war heroes seemed to be finding themselves at the end of the line, criticized by everyone who opposed the war in Viet Nam. I became frustrated by the thought of spending the next four years of my life fighting for a cause that just didn't sit right with me. The only hope I had was to quietly do my time. Time was one thing I had plenty of, so I decided to make the best of it.

Looking back, I remember distinctly how I first became aware of martial arts. During a sixty-day stretch at sea flying sorties off the coast to northern targets in Viet Nam, I emerged from the carrier's movie theater. A shipmate of mine, Ben, had just come back from the gym. Ben stopped me in the narrow passageway and said, "Jack, you told me you wanted to learn martial arts someday and I found a master-at-arms first class who does just that each day. His name is Love, and he teaches under the flight deck in a storage room when time permits."

"Thanks, Ben," I said. A small spark of fire seemed to ignite in my heart.

I spent the next day looking for that master-at-arms and a glimmer of hope entered my dismal world as my quest began. That same afternoon, I found Mr. Love and the sanctuary where he taught Chinese *kempo*. Strange as it seemed, Mr. Love's shipboard *dojo* was located under the flight deck wing where the sound of arresting gear clattered and echoed. The arresting gear strained as it angrily snagged the landing aircraft returning from missions. In life you often find what you need in the strangest places. I stepped in the door to find this southern black belt clad in his *keikogi* (uniform) with the emblem of the *kempo karate* system, "Love's Chinese Kempo Karate" attached to his *uwagi* (uniform top).

Through the doorway, I watched a class and *kata* (forms) practice for over an hour before being asked to enter and sit for a while. Mr. Love moved through the *dojo* with the grace of a dancer while giving instruction to students. I caught glimpses of hand techniques that struck targets with lightning speed. *This is it,* I told myself, *now I can find a way out of my regrettable mindset.* A strong feeling of purpose immediately filled me. I knew that this instant would serve to show me the means to seek my higher self and never feel the unwelcome solitude again. Martial arts would be my friend and companion. Here, surrounded by steel in the bleak light, a special bright fulfilling essence glowed, and I began to hope for the best Mr. Love could show me in his expertise.

After a brief introduction, Mr. Love invited me into the makeshift *dojo* and began to explain the structured workouts, the group training he used, and the theory behind Chinese *kempo karate.* As a novice, I questioned less his ability (though I figured it to be superb), but more how I could learn this esoteric art and find a mechanism to release my inner emotions. I wondered at his mastery and the mystery behind the ways of Eastern martial arts. My desire to learn became more intense with each question I asked myself. It was the quintessence of Mr. Love's demeanor, the pure martial arts attraction, and the spirit I perceived in this little *dojo* that drew me deeper into the modern practice of ancient unarmed combat.

I had heard of unique *dojo*s in Japan and even read of them after purchasing books on the subject, so my knowledge was book-acquired at best. Unknown to me at the time, I would ultimately travel to Japan, which would nurture the seeds of universal prosperity for a lifelong study of the Way.

The draw of the *dojo* itself was not the beauty of the grand practice halls of Japan or Hong Kong, but it was what you accepted as the way place, the means to an enlightened end. The functional stage was set, and the aesthetic value of the martial arts is expressed in the unity of the performer or practitioner and his skill. We practiced on floors not made of highly polished oak or exotic woven-straw *tatami* mats, but of warship grey steel covered every two or three feet with non-skid woven into the surface of the ship's skin to prevent a painful fall. Steel beams covered the width of the room, supporting the flight deck, and small four-foot watertight doorways separated the three contiguous compartments that were fast becoming my new home away from home. *Kiai*s (spirit yells) found in martial art systems filled each room as students practiced their specific ritualistic forms and techniques.

In the center room, several students gathered in a tight circle, holding a formal sitting position while two would-be warriors squared off and began *kumite* (free sparring). Mr. Love controlled the action. Other students surrounding the two opponents were there not only to observe, but to serve as a protective barrier between the fighters and the steel wall, lest they collide with it in the heat of battle. This seated position during *kumite* allowed those watching to observe, analyze, and respond quickly to the raging battle before them. Legs normally became cramped from sitting in this position, but over time the body learned to adjust. Learning was born of observation, experience, and study. From time to time, I heard of a strange practice in an area called the "Iron Box" but would not understand its brutal truth until much later.

I became amazed at how these *karateka* trained in their off time from whatever task they were trained to perform on board for the war. It at first seemed inconceivable how the concentration was maintained while the clash and clatter of war took place during the flight operations directly above. War was constantly a heartbeat away. Death too was near. Only recently, a shipmate had been crushed by a 500-pound bomb rolling out of control on the flight deck. Another had been taken by an F-4 Phantom jet that exploded while landing on the return from a mission over northern Viet Nam. Several flight crew airmen were injured in the incident. Most of the gut-wrenching news drifted up from sick bay or someone starting a chain of rumors. The flight deck of an aircraft carrier had to be one of the most hazardous places to work in the world. A *kiai* rang out just as a point was scored.

Two other students somehow practiced throws against the steel decks, careful to avoid a full-power execution. I heard that *tatami* mats had been ordered for the Kempo Club and were expected to arrive when the ship returned to Nippon (Japan). The rooms and floor shook with each aircraft launch, but the class continued without interruption. "Form! Form! Watch your form," yelled Mr. Love, who now intensively hammered the two boys in *kumite*. "Focus, focus on your intentions." I was asked by Mr. Love if I would like to train in *kempo karate* and answered, "May I come all the time?"

Mr. Love's comment was, "Only if you want to find the real *Budo*." Somewhat confused about the meaning of *Budo,* I answered, "I'll do whatever it takes, Mr. Love."

He responded, "By the way, I am 'sensei' to you now." The word stuck instantly in my mind. Now I had a *sensei* to follow. Life would never be the same.

As I looked over his shoulder at the training taking place, a student executed a barrage of kicks and punches all discharged in a furious attack just as an F-4 Phantom took off on the forward flight deck overhead. Everything shook once again and seemed to be in harmony with both the attacker and the launch. Their universal energy and the war machine blended. It seemed this would be my escape from the adverse feelings of the Viet Nam War and a new path to follow for the remaining two or three years. I looked around—steel at every turn, hot rivets forced into beams of steel in the birth of this massive giant. Watertight hatches ensured integrity and were closed, fastened, and sealed during general quarters. Colors were always the same: bleak grey steel wall to wall with the inner deck we practiced on, which was rust-color red. No doubt it would be useful in hiding the distinct color of blood.

Time in its usual sense seemed to crawl by as we counted the days before we reached the next port for R & R or the time when we would be going home, never to return to this strange and dangerous land. Thoughts danced in the corners of my mind as to how skillful a martial artist I could become. Everything spun and everything excited me. The desire burned in me to attack, defend, throw, and ward off as many as ten attackers in a fury at my command. It was only the beginning, and the intense training was still to come.

Months passed as my character and temperament were shaped and reshaped into a more secure and determined human being. Never can I recall any boredom in the thousands of techniques I continuously drilled during my newfound journey. Practice became breakfast, lunch, and dinner, holding me at each moment.

Now the Philippine port drew near. Over the loudspeakers came the command for those of us picked for the first shore duty to prepare ourselves. I looked on from high above as the behemoth aircraft carrier was slowly forced into position next to the huge pier. Contact was made with personnel on the pier, and those assigned to secure the ship immediately put three- and four-inch lines securely in place to hold the monster during its stay in port. More ammunition stood waiting on the dock. Supplies stacked ten feet high were patiently waiting to be loaded on the ship. I gazed out over the base where various types of transportation busily moved around, ready to transfer the sailors and Marines into town. I wasted no time in preparing to go ashore.

Sensei invited me to go into town with him for the night to have dinner at a restaurant which he had frequented over the years. This would be an honor. I left my berthing quarters and met Sensei at the gangway. Earlier he had told me to bring my practice uniform *(keikogi)* whenever I went ashore with him. He asked, "Did you forget your uniform?"

"No Sensei, it's ready for me."

He smiled and said, "Lets go nail a couple walls." I could only wonder at the meaning of his comment and what this fateful day held in store for me.

Much of what I was acquiring was without doubt new to me. I was privileged to be taken under Sensei's wing to learn and grasp at the straws because I was sent to the master-at-arms force on the ship to serve in a policing role. There your uniforms were pressed, you gained first place in the food line, and everything generally went easier for you. Fate brought me close to this mentor and he seemed to see something special in my spirit as I hammered away during all the practice sessions. It wasn't long before I earned a special respect from training and the honor of being in his presence. Everyone knew that the lean black martial artist who was "lifer" material for the U.S. Navy was not to be fooled with.

Sensei Love had shown me his certificates of grade *(menjo),* and lately his fifth-grade black belt level *menjo* for Chinese *kempo karate* earned from a Japanese-American *sensei* in Hawaii. I wondered whether the day would come for me to receive my black belt. However, time would be limited over the next two years. I would attempt as usual to practice heart and soul, day in and day out.

I noticed Sensei Love's hands. They looked like hammers, and his knuckles were enlarged from punching the ancient *makiwara* (a striking post used to strengthen body parts and support the harmonizing of mind-body-spirit through repetition). There was one unique room where we practiced special martial arts drills. It was a very rough, pitted, and jagged area of steel deck, sprayed with a vinegar solution each time we used it and then lightly sprinkled with salt. We fought our pain while doing knuckle push-ups in such a crude way. Skin turned red and painful at first, but over time, calluses began to form, wrist strength increased, backs became stronger, and spirits grew self-consuming. Sensei always placed two carving knives, blades up, in a rack that kept them fixed in place at a point below your stomach so as to force you to do what he demanded. Never a dull moment, you might say.

We jumped into the first cab and headed into town. Driving through the base, we passed the officers club, base recreation hall, and many ships in port taking on supplies and provisions. As we passed through the guard gate, the MP smiled sarcastically and said, "Have fun, boys, it's going to be a great day." It was common for new sailors and Marines to go to the beach in town for a great time and return the same night drunk, broke, or mugged from unpredictable encounters with the locals, bar girls, or each other. I had witnessed this far too many times in the past, and with my newfound martial arts role model, I knew things would be very different. Ethical standards based on time-honored traditions were going to keep me in check and acutely aware of the way I carried myself.

I came to find out later that the base has an island for servicemen to enjoy the hospitality of the Philippines without risking the normal brawls, mugging, and conflict. Thinking back, it was the one we passed steaming into Subic Bay.

Quickly we made our way into the town of Olongapo. About midway through the cluster of redundant shacks and rows of bars, we stopped and left the cab. Sensei first wanted to get some lunch at an old hang-out he frequented while in port. I followed him through the maze of twisted steel-fabricated structures, muddy streets, and paths, then into a garden in front of an amazing Gothic-style house. The house appeared broken down and very old. I marveled about this first mission for food and where it had led us.

Eyes seemed to focus on our company as though we were intruding onto some ancient sacred ground. Stepping among many Filipinos attempting to escape the afternoon heat on the steps and wooden porch, we entered the house. By now I was soaking wet from the intense humidity always found in the tropical jungles. I was ready for a swim. My freshly pressed service uniform looked as if it had been through a street battle, without a single dry spot to be found.

To my surprise, Sensei was greeted by an old friend who seated us in a corner and mentioned that she knew exactly what he wanted, "the usual." Sensei asked me, "Do you like chicken fried rice?" Without ever sampling it before, I honorably agreed. Soon I found myself looking at a pile of rice loaded with morsels of stir-fried chicken, local vegetables, and exotic fruit as side dishes spread in front of me. It was difficult to imagine this meal fit for a king in such a shabby atmosphere. Digging in, I asked myself what could be next, when four San Miguel beers hit the table chilled in ice with much condensation running down the side. Being in this strange land was made stranger by the intense 99 degree heat, rickety furnishings, windows without glass, old wooden floors, and the girls who filled the room. We kept eating and drinking.

As I ate, my eyes scanned the room for available exits in case Sensei and I had to escape. Call it common sense or fear, I wanted to be fully prepared for whatever might happen. While eating, Sensei said, "Relax, it's O.K. This is where I usually meet a local *sifu* (martial arts master) in a form of *gung fu*. By the way, don't stuff yourself, we are going to his *dojo* in a couple of hours and will train in the Philippine sunshine. I forgot to tell you, no girls today. We train only, then tonight drink some green beer and go back to the ship. Tomorrow it's in-country for more practice."

Finishing the excellent meal and a few more beers, Sensei started telling me of his adventures in the Philippines. Most of his battle engagements occurred in the usual bars and watering holes where strobe lights and 60s rock-and-roll music filled the air. It was remarkable to go into some nightclub here and listen to local groups mimic closely the sounds of Motown favorites or California rock groups singing the old tunes everyone knows. Finding myself thousands of miles from home was disagreeable, so beer and music filled the gaps over the long lonely hours. Growing up with close friends and buddies made it challenging at times to be surrounded by Marines and sailors from the Bronx, Chicago, Miami, Dallas, or Anytown, U.S.A. Each had a different manner, a new or old story to tell, and a life to which they desired to return.

Sensei regaled me with tales of at least a dozen battles over the next two hours before we left for the *dojo*. My mind was filled with memories of his encounters as I paid the bill with local money obtained earlier. A heavy downpour of rain ended as we left, and we were able to cool off for a brief moment. The large leaves of exotic banana trees dripped as streams of water uncontrollably ran around the trunks. Children played in the mud-colored water and relentlessly pushed us for a handout. Quickly winding our way back to the main boulevard, we flagged down a taxi and off we went once again. Traffic was jammed up constantly, so it was often better to walk everywhere. The benefit of riding was not being harassed by the panhandlers, which was a constant ordeal when in town. I looked at other faces in the heat, many already drunk from the effects of the green San Miguel beer colliding with the sun. Nightfall would soon arrive and that would be the time to experience enough nightlife and insanity at the local saloons to satisfy anybody.

"Stop at the next corner," Sensei said. Rounding a bend in the road, we jumped out of the jeep-style taxi. A few buildings stood out among the bars on the outskirts of town. Once again, I felt the eyes of others staring at us as intruders from another planet. Peddlers at fruit stands and shops with consumer wares seemed unaccustomed to seeing American faces. I asked Sensei if we were safe around here and he said as long as it's daylight. With that comforting thought, I glanced at my watch then looked at the sun. He told me to stay close to him. I did!

We next approached a two-story building and entered a flimsy stairway that bridged a small creek. Prior to entering the stairway, I noticed Chinese *kanji* (characters) written across the overhang. There underneath the *kanji* were the English words "Chinese Gung Fu." As we continued around the building on the makeshift walkway, I clung to the wall because the floor felt old, rotten, and rickety. I was sure that with one false move, I'd find myself immersed in the deep, stagnant swamp water and local sewage down below. By the way, the sewers in Olongapo were the streets, alleys, and back windows. No conveniences to be found; only nature's immediate necessities. I looked up and noticed a couple of windows on the second floor with kids hanging out of them. Strange as it may seem, things were much quieter than you would expect and, to say the least, somehow unsettling. Laundry was strung between the buildings and litter was everywhere. I watched several old women dressed in black huddled in a circle chanting in some ritual common to the area. I didn't know what it meant, but I hoped it wasn't a prayer for Sensei and me.

As we stepped around the end of the structure and out of the shade, the rays of the afternoon sun pierced our bodies like spears. In front of us was a door slightly ajar. We stopped. To my right across a small river of sludge and swamp were fields thickly covered with palms, bamboo, and sugar cane. *Who was watching us from within the thicket?* I asked myself. I would have felt better had I carried my 45-caliber automatic pistol in my belt, but then I remembered Sensei was here. That was much better than a clip of the eight powerful rounds. I was startled to hear a *kiai* (spirit yell) blast from inside. Just then a smile came across Sensei's face as someone familiar stepped out of the doorway to meet us.

A lean tall Filipino dressed in a *karate keikogi* greeted Sensei and me. "Sailor *sensei*," he said, and Sensei introduced me to Mr. Chuck Sifu. He said, "Call me Chuck Sifu, or just plain Chuck." Removing our mud-covered shoes, we stepped up a few steps and entered the *dojo*. The small entrance area, called *genkan* in *Nihongo* (Japanese) had a different name in Chinese or Filipino, which now evades me. I noticed the mixture of races and wondered how it might influence the training. We always seem to look at things from a modern American point of view, so learning to adjust to a new culture and ethic was confusing, to say the least. I followed Sensei and placed my shoes in an area made for them.

I noticed a cockroach charge full-speed across the shoe boxes and disappear down a hole. Was his fear my shoes and the giant intruding in his domain or did he suspect some type of warfare about to shake the building? A doubt hung in my mind as to whether the building would stay upright on its stilts if battle became too intense.

Looking around I noticed three students who had just come to practice stepping into the training area wearing their white *keikogi*. They strode past me expressing an arrogant attitude then moved to the back of the *dojo*. On the left side of their *keikogi* I recognized Chinese or Japanese characters *(moji)* and a translation that read "Chinese Gung Fu." I believe a crane and snake had been embroidered on the lapels as well.

I had read that many of the Shaolin Temple teachings were passed on to those who traveled to China seeking knowledge. They brought back to the Philippines and Okinawa the martial arts expertise sometimes called *wu shu*. From its foothold in China, martial arts traveled to Taiwan, Nippon (Japan), and Korea. History was not my mainstay at the time but free-sparring was, and I had been training hard over the last six months. One thing is certain, history has a tendency to repeat itself, so one needs to become familiar with the past.

Almost a year into *kempo* I had suffered the pains of contact, the throws against the steel floor, and the challenge of adversity from my teacher's ways. In the Shaolin Temple one learned various forms of White Crane, Eagle Claw, Leopard, and Tiger styles. Sensei had mentioned the Praying Mantis style and that it may be a part of this school found in the Jook Lum Monastery in Guandong Province.

Many of the Chinese systems include not only self-defense as their main objective, but also the healing arts—*ming gong, shen gong* (spirit style), and *qi gong* (internal power of martial arts). At any rate, teachings and traditions tend to get lost due to distance and time from teacher to teacher. I did not know if these practitioners were loyal to any one cause in the form of honorable lineage or whether they took anything new that came along. I found the latter was more important.

Sifu Chuck asked us to sit down for a while until he and a couple of his students were finished with some *kata*.

Sensei and I found a place to sit and watch. Crossed-legged *(agura)*, I made myself as comfortable as possible in the intense humidity and looked over this strange training hall. I first noticed the unusual floor. Long planks of dark Philippine wood ran lengthwise from the back to the front. Stained and polished to a very high sheen, the floor appeared to be slippery, but not so as the students went from movement to movement. Amazingly enough, the inside of the *dojo* was indeed a beautiful sight to behold. It was apparent that those who belonged were proud of their school and the one who led them.

The cracks where the planks in the floor touched were honed to a fine radius so that no one would cut their feet. I gathered that beneath the boards was reinforcement because the wood gave in unison. I only wondered where one would end up if the floor fell through. Underneath the floor was the unknown darkness of marsh and decay.

Everything was dark to create a cool atmosphere from the intense heat raging outside in the savage sun. Sweat streamed down my chest and onto my stomach. I moved my hands from my thighs to find wet fingerprints where they had been. I noticed Sensei intensely focused on a shrine in the back of the *dojo*. He too was beginning to sweat, and no words had yet passed from either of our lips. I had numerous questions, but held my silence. For some reason he looked bigger, more massive than when we first came through the door. Our senses seemed to get keener as the feeling of distant warfare approached our souls. I came to realize it was nature's way of making battle preparations.

Hanging above the ceiling were old Casablanca fans turning at slow speed as if to keep cool the spider webs that were spun close to the ceiling. Beams ran from wall to wall high above planks which held the metal paneling outside as a roof. Only three windows lined the outside wall. Things were different here, as I was learning quickly. Everything is always wet from a tropical downpour, the frustrating annoyance of mosquitoes constantly swarming about, and tempers were tested, cut short, at each moment in the struggle to survive. I believe the discipline served as a relief from the atmosphere one had to survive day in and day out.

Many hidden outposts among the dense forests and coastal regions of the Philippine Islands held small *dojos* from various styles of *karate-do, gung fu, gong fu, tai chi chuan,* etc., all with the same purpose—to find the real self and obsess into the mysterious world of secret unarmed combat. Whether it was a Chen style or a *taiji* master's watered-down form of self-defense, each in its own way served the sanctuary of inner peace.

In the far corner sat two large clay barrels. They must have weighed hundreds of pounds, as both were approximately three feet tall and a couple feet in diameter. On the sides were beautiful gold Chinese dragons painted carefully in a circling manner. The clay background was painted or tinted a deep lacquer black, making the gold dragons appear to jump out at you. Down one side Chinese *kanji* were distinctively written to remind the students of the tasks which no doubt related to their ordeals and the cultivation of skill within their honorable system.

Following *kata* practice, Sifu Chuck brought us over to the so-called special training clay barrels and showed us his distinct practice method. Each was filled with a mixture of pebbles that looked as if they were all ground in a specific way that made each pebble sharp.

Driving one's spear hand into the midst of the large clay barrels seemed simple enough, but when Sifu Chuck asked me to attempt it, I found out my skin was sensitive and soft. The semi-sharp pebbles cut and stung with repeated contact. I imagined the strength one could gain as I observed the callused look on both of Sifu's hands. He then drove his punching fist several times into the center, driving the stones to the side from the blast and quickly replacing the hole left behind as he pulled it away. I noticed the momentary twist of his fist when buried deep within the mixture, no doubt to work larger portions of his fist. I was impressed to see that his entire knuckle area and forefist were a mass of calluses.

I quickly thought of a way to propose the same use on the ship and briefly discussed it with Sensei later. It wasn't until several months later that we constructed our own special training barrels on the ship, but instead of using stones, we secretly made a purchase from a machinist mate who worked in the engine room—hundreds of steel ball bearings. Bartering was the only way to survive in the military. This allowed many of the same training secrets found that day in the *gung fu dojo* to be useful. Sensei would trade American things and knowledge in return.

Facing the front of the *dojo* I noticed a Chinese hanging scroll and next to it a large photo of the master of the *dojo.* Observing all of the Chinese broadswords, I assumed that this style was close to the *wu shu* style because of the many *kata,* but then many different systems of martial arts had their own *kata.* I had to wait. The hanging scrolls were about seven feet high and three feet apart, stretching from ceiling to floor. The black silk with Chinese *kanji* reflected a serene and beautiful image as the broadswords menacingly loomed over them on either side.

After watching Sifu finish a very lengthy form, all his students departed except for one. Sensei and I were directed to change into our *keikogi* and warm up. We exited the main room and found a small changing room. The bathroom actually hung out over and beyond the outside wall with the creek running below. No doubt where the water and waste products ended up. I observed the outline of the bathroom and changing area, scanning carefully for any deadly tropical spiders between the cracks. Then we quickly changed and prepared for our entrance back into the training hall. The smell of mildew filled the stale and motionless air. No matter how glassy the *dojo* floor may look, or how uniform the appearance of weapons hanging on the side wall, you could never get rid of—let alone get used to—that mildew smell moving through the air and into your lungs.

Sensei told me to follow him, say nothing, and act formidable. "If I have you free-spar *kumite,*" he said, "do not kill anyone with your short temper." A short temper was one of my weak points, and patience was a virtue I had little of. It always provided a way to get me into trouble, especially when opening my big mouth. I answered quietly, "I understand, Sensei." We walked over to the weapons wall, which seemed to hold both Okinawan as well as Chinese *chuan fa* weaponry. *bo,* spears, and Chinese-style *nunchaku* with three sectional pieces clung to the wooden wall. I noticed the broadsword weapons to be dull but well dented. Perhaps used often, they found contact a mighty force in this *dojo* or perhaps they were used to fillet fish when hunger took over. At any rate, I knew that a good show or lesson may come from this system of Southern and Northern Shaolin (Silum) *gung fu,* whichever it was. I was confused and reluctant to ask for fear of embarrassing Sensei.

As we stretched, I noticed Sifu do a stretch I'd never seen before. He moved to the wall and leaned one side of his body against it, then with little effort drew his lead knee up to his chest without arching into it with his body. Then to my astonishment, he extended the rest of his leg by unfolding it so that it pointed straight up past his face. There, he locked the joint out completely without any effort. He was actually in a position looking out level with his knee next to his eyes. The splits standing upright. Under my skin, I flipped out. It was apparent that he spent a few hours of his life everyday stretching, or perchance he took ballet at an early age. Not likely!

Next Sensei and Sifu went off to a corner of the *dojo* and began to discuss *kata* and *waza* (technique). I was instructed to practice one-step free-sparring in position with Sifu's brown belt. I knew the purpose here was to feel him out for power and effectiveness. You can find out a great deal about another's prowess during the methodical contact exchanged back and forth while engaged in this practice.

I thought back to the ship *dojo* where I and another training partner used arm-hardening techniques to solidify the arms. I believe this is referred to as *kotekitai* in *Nihongo*. One of Sensei's students was a welder on board the aircraft carrier. Sensei had designed a striking device and instructed the student to construct it in a specific way— a type of striking base for elbows and hands or feet that clamped to the iron beams in our training space. It could be rigged in any space that had beams, and all did. Four steel springs on the corners found their place between the bolts and the beam, therefore allowing any contact made to be absorbed into the springs only slightly. The plate was approximately eight by twelve inches. On its surface was a canvas pad approximately two inches thick backed with hard padding and glued to the plate with rubber cement. I first noticed a student using it at one of the practice sessions; he was breaking the device in while attacking the target with elbow strikes. To my surprise, he struck it over a thousand times and repeated the exercise at the end of practice.

This student had been with Sensei for more than two years and mentioned that there was a solution he used on his elbows that Sensei had prepared in the ship's kitchen. The solution was a Chinese or Japanese herb mixture for the purpose of creating calluses and overcoming bruising. As he pulled his *keikogi* sleeve up, I observed an elongated knot that ran the length of his forearm from elbow to wrist. It was hard as iron and callused from repetitive use. He said, "This is one of my favorite striking techniques." He demonstrated to me how he applied the strike when engaged in a grappling position and subsequently laid his forearm into a steel wall just to exhibit the solution's usefulness.

Later I found out how formidable this unique personal weapon was during a free-sparring session. Shortly afterward, Sensei began the same instructional process with me. Much later, we started using arm-pounding techniques against one another in a striking fashion. This type of practice Sensei told me was carried out in a style called *Uechi-Ryu* in Okinawa, as well as in many old Chinese systems of combat.

Sensei trained often in private, and I could only imagine the power found in his technique and spirit when he exhibited them during combative engagement with us. It always seemed his fix was to fight three or five of us at a time. Fists and feet flew everywhere and so did we during *kumite*.

I caught my wind during one-step sparring to observe Sensei going through a Chinese *kempo kata* I had never witnessed before. Slowly spinning on the glossy dark wooden floors, he glided like a leopard on the stalk. Arms rose and fell in a swift movement as though a storm were about to explode. Up into the air he went, striking in two directions at imaginary opponents, then he rolled into a supple ball as he made contact with the floor. As he circled rhythmically, I noticed something beginning to happen. So absorbed was my intensive observation that I began to see the attackers coming at him from every direction, each one falling aside as he moved in a fury in multiple directions, then froze until the next wave of destruction was encountered.

The storm was engaged one moment, then became calm with regulated breathing the next, then the action repeated, followed by lightning charges or blocking alternatives in a variety of methods. His *kiai* rang out as a powerful stomp collided with the wooden *dojo* floor. I saw parrots and other tropical birds scatter outside the window and disappear into the palms and thicket. In a dazzling display of *ki* (inner strength), Sensei jumped into the air once again, driving a back kick into space, landing on his fists and toes in a push-up position. Then he rose and bowed.

My heart seemed to hesitate, then, as with all tropical storms, another downpour began to fall outside in the humid atmosphere. Everything seemed to reflect motionless for a brief significant instant. The awnings outside the windows streamed with water like miniature waterfalls, Sensei was drenched in sweat, my arms were pounding from contact, and my shins screamed as blood seeped from an old wound earned on the ship. This was the active moment of Zen for us all. We as *karateka* would attempt to melt and blend with it.

Sensei glared at me so I continued my practice. Reluctantly, I woke up looking for more inner strength and found what I needed. My training partner asked permission to relieve himself. Sifu grunted and hesitantly allowed it. I worked on my breathing while Sifu exchanged a *kata* and ideas with Sensei. It was common for visitors of one style to teach specific *kata* in exchange for others. Sensei told me once that one should promise much and hold the prize. I understood what he meant. Never show all your cards even if you're going to lose. One has to take risks, as life is for us all, and work his strategy if he is to win, even if it is at another time and place.

I noticed several children watching from outside the doors in the back of the *dojo*. At my first observation when we all started there were only two, but now perhaps twelve or thirteen young boys and girls focused their gaze upon us. Dressed poorly and standing in the lukewarm rain, they were soaking wet, but all stood quietly and motionless. No doubt Sifu would throw them all into the slimy creek if one were to utter a sound. I assumed this was a common discipline for the privilege of observing ancient rituals. I heard him say later that many a young boy wanted to join, but he was refused for several months before Sifu allowed the "newborn" to come in as a junior and begin cleaning tasks on the road to full acceptance and training. That practice is something the Japanese still do today in many of the older-style *dojo*s.

Sad as it may seem, I wondered how many children, not even ten or eleven years of age, lived in the streets attempting to make it on their own. I looked to the right and saw a spider the size of my fist climb the wall. Slowly he climbed to the highest level, occasionally swinging from web to web until he stopped to investigate some trapped prey and the activity taking place below. How poetic, I thought. Apparently, his home was the *dojo* and no one forced him to move out. The thought of combat in the insect world crossed my mind. Vigilance at every turn.

My legs immediately felt new strength enter and I waited for my next combative venture to unfold. My partner soon returned, and we both were told to move the center of the *dojo* floor for *kumite*. As we stood facing one another, Sifu brought what appeared to be some line or rope to the center. Sifu Chuck spoke first, "Perhaps your Sensei did not mention a new training format we would initiate you with today." No doubt this was some ancient method of building perseverance in the pupil as he progressed over the years, if he survived. Sensei grabbed some line and helped Sifu tie our wrists together in front of us, so we were unable to use our punching skills or blocks in any decisive manner. This meant uncontrolled balance and a strange new feeling of uneasiness which rolled deep down in my guts. The wrists were tied loose enough so that you could twist or position your stance and grab with your fingers or use an awkward cross block for kicks, although I doubted if much of the slack would serve to be any support.

In fact, as I waited for my *aite* (opponent) to prepare, I quickly began to think of various ways to conform. What variety of tactics could I put into play? I was always taught to improvise during boot camp. In what could be a brutal realization, I now did just that.

I analyzed all my options. I had double arm blocks, cross blocks for defense against kicks, and the same thing available for punch attacks. I knew I must absorb specific attacks in order to deflect and counter. I knew not what our teacher's requests were going to be nor our fate. I moved around a moment finding new ways to use my elbows or legs for blocking or counterattacking. Knees are formidable weapons, and I thought of ways to use these inside weapons, as we would most likely engage in a grappling battle.

Next, Sensei commanded us to sit in the formal position *(seiza)* to meditate before our *kumite.* This was the first time I would encounter this method of free-sparring. I meditated for the moment. I looked down at the floor as sweat dripped off my head onto the dark glistening ebony boards. As I drifted, I heard the sound of U.S. Air Force jets flying overhead, then the rain began to stop. Briefly, rays of sun streamed through various holes and cracks in the wall and open windows. For an instant, I noticed the light reflect on the weapons wall and hit a broadsword, redirecting the sunlight to my eyes. I saw spots glitter momentarily and closed my eyes to readjust and gain focus. Perhaps some sign? I wasn't sure. More sweat ran down my temples as I lost track of each second.

My mind became reminiscent of "monkey-mind," random thoughts scattering about. *Concentrate,* I told myself, *this is war! Focus, for God's sake, and get it together!* Fear is an emotion, the worst emotion forcing a blind man into deeper fear. *Kill the emotion, you kill the fear,* I told myself. I made a firm resolution: I would bring forth the animal instinct I had learned to harness and do away with this challenger. Failure would not conquer me. It would not defeat me if I had the determination to succeed.

My heart began to pound as I started to pump up the inner volume—tense like a young rooster and hungry as a lion in the forest. Blood now forced itself to all the required organs, based on the survival instinct. I knew I was representing my teacher, a master in his own right, and I wasn't about to let him down.

We both were instructed to rise and stand facing one another. I looked deep into my opponent's inscrutable eyes and smiled briefly inside my head. *You are no more than a heavy bag, a figment of my imagination,* I told myself. My fear seemed to subside. I shook with the thrill of the attack. My hunger for victory possessed every muscle readied for action. Now fear was replaced with a sense of unstoppable victory. I sought the pure genius of whatever my past could supply me with in this time. Both Sensei and Sifu positioned each of us ready to begin.

"You will both use whatever means available to score in full-power attacks to win." The line became taut and every muscle screamed to explode. Ready, bow, begin! I knew his vague weaknesses from our one-on-one step practice, but also knew many seasoned technicians do not give up all their secrets. I threw caution to the wind. *You only die once,* I told myself, *so the hell with it.* Holding my guard close with cover I attacked first, then we clashed as knees and kicks flew. I found all kick attacks coming in relatively awkwardly with our hands loosely bound, and the counterattacks as well became the kicking weapons attempting to find their mark somewhere in the area of my upper body or head. Blocking with both arms as planned, I power-blocked each kick and slipped to the side during each assault. With each kick, the line pulled my block from my guarded position, but I resisted in like manner.

I tied up briefly, trapping at first to sweep his leg sharply but missed, then I struck upward with both fists to find contact with his solar plexus. At last success tasted sweet.

He dropped to the floor in a heap. Sensei thundered at me to hold my ground as I started to stomp-kick his head. Starting to attack was a difficult undertaking when feeling out a worthy opponent, but stopping in the heat of battle was even more arduous. Your juices are flowing, your *ki* is equivalent to pure oxygen, and your fighting spirit is formidable. I held my ground momentarily to catch my breath, sat in *seiza* while still watching my opponent, and anticipated the next command. "Center!" Sifu shouted. Back to the center we rushed ungracefully and stood once again on guard, motionless, chests heaving, eyes burning to defend honor. I knew this was now more than a learning experience. It was a test of our martial arts systems and styles on a combative level and a reflection of our respective *senseis'* expert guidance and teaching in unconquerable spirit. I was to yield to no man, and destiny would find me victorious.

"Hajime!" (Begin!) Sensei commanded. My opponent launched a furious attack. I stepped back and off to the side. In an explosive blur of kicks—front kicks, side kicks, hooking Chinese-style kicks—my opponent continued to advance as if expecting to force his victory. I was constantly moving, sliding and slipping the assault, hoping that he would blow out like a spent candle. I sensed his approaching exhaustion. Suddenly and defiantly, I stood my ground. I jammed his roundhouse kick with a *kiai* and locked the line in position. Releasing his kick, I held on tightly to his *keikogi,* squeezing forcibly with the left hand on the shoulder area. I then slammed my right elbow into his chest, then again up to his head. Hands fastening in position with resistance, I threw elbow after elbow. Hanging on, he tried to smother the attack, but several blows slammed his midsection. Once again, my elbows found their mark. Now exchanging blows, his right knee found my rib cage. I tried desperately to gain my air, hung on, and for a moment almost dropped. Spinning around several times, we both hit the wall next to one of the windows. No one attempted to halt our battle.

Still holding fast, I matched his knee kicks and smashed into his quadricep, attempting to break his stance and hold. He faltered and we both went down engaged and rolling. *"Matte! Matte!"* Stop, back to the center. Sifu examined the bloody nose my head had crashed into and my badly bruised cheekbone, but no broken bones—at least that's what I was led to believe. Stoicism was a must, never give in to your injury. At that point of observation, pain shot through my rib cage once again. I had fractured something, but now was not the time for analysis.

We readied ourselves once again, both with heaving chests, our wrists now red and ripped from the line. Center, ready, *hajime.* Agony, distress, and injuries were once again forgotten. Less movement this time accompanied our battle plans. This time I knew his injuries. This time he would fall in a final confrontation. I was going after his knees. Forward and back, side to side, I rolled my upper body looking for the right moment, the correct movement to set the *aite* up for strategy. He goaded me on, but I ignored his ploy. Snapping the line between my wrists, giving and losing ground, I would not become frustrated. Once I began strategy, it would change in an instant. As he dropped into a deep-ground type stance, I found the response to be pure *gung fu,* and I gleamed at my thoughts momentarily. The ground is good only when I find it by mistake and must escape. Attempting to attack from such a low position is weak and rarely effective. This was yet to be found.

Four feet of distance hung between us, yet neither one of us attempted to choke or rip with the line as a weapon, likely a successful move, but an unhonorable one.

In the *dojo* we practiced occasionally on our backs and sides from the deck. From this position we learned to respond by swiftly sweeping using kicks or escaping in a manner to evade the enemy. The saying "once you're down, you're down" is true for the most part. Grappling, or *katame waza* in Japanese, is essential to survival. Embraced in a battle position with a fellow student, one had to escape his hold and counterattack. Not always a simple task to do, as nature forces us to hold on to things for safety. Breaking away—*hazushi-waza,* or escaping techniques—always left one *aite* scoring to win, as the first one out of the gate had the odds.

In a final charge, my opponent attempted to sweep me from the ground level. I jumped and landed with both feet on his ankle partly by mistake and partly on purpose. Something crunched loudly. As he staggered to a standing attack position, I covered with both arms tied together close in and slammed my roundhouse kick into his knee. Down he went, but to my surprise he rose once again. We both found ourselves in a grappling attitude again, and in one final attempt I cross-grabbed his lapels with each hand on opposite sides frustrated from bound wrists, drove my hip into his midsection while spinning inside and sideways, swept, and threw with a *kiai.* I bent deep in the knees, exhaled sharply in the motion, squeezed with all the force my hands could grip, and using a hip throw sent him sailing through the air. His tall body came down followed by his legs as if in slow motion. As he smashed the floor I heard a loud crack!

His eyes rolled as he went out for a moment, then reaching for his shoulder, he writhed in pain. As the moments passed I felt success flow through my body, but an emotion of concern followed for my fighting partner. Sifu and Sensei rushed to help him back to his senses. He forced a partial smile and I knew the battle for victory had been laid to rest. I had always thrown my partners with care while in the ship *dojo,* much aware of the hard steel surfaces able to inflict considerable damage. This time, I held back nothing. To my amazement I noticed the wooden floor had broken. The perfect wooden plank where his shoulder made contact cracked and then broke under the impact. Part of the plank hung down below, and one could observe the gloomy depths of the tropical snake-ridden sludge below. Most of the buildings I noticed were built off the ground due to tropical rains and inclement weather. The *gung fu dojo* was no exception. This floor would need a temporary overhaul.

I could only think of what was going through Sifu's mind, as he seemed to cringe when he noticed the damage. Repairs were costly, but more importantly, the excuse his student would have to give to other students was the most frustrating thought. It would be a memory I was sure would serve to haunt the mind of a vanquished warrior. I asked myself what lay in store for he who fails. Failure breeds awakening if one isn't dead.

I rose and bowed honorably in respect of my opponent, my task, my style, and my battle.

It was soon afterward in the midst of more San Miguel beer and broiled fish that we discussed the different practice methods and experimentation with the stone-filled barrels. Interested as I may have been, my injuries subdued my excitement and effort to test them full power.

In Sifu's small office overlooking the busy sidestreet below, I was presented a brown belt as honorary reward for winning my stoic battle. The belt, which is called an *obi* in Japanese, was covered with Chinese writing and handmade to be soft and silky. I looked at Sensei, who smiled and approved my accepting it as a token of honor. I placed it at my side and bowed respectfully, attempting not to show the pain that filled my side from fractured ribs or the shin bruises that were swelling and becoming intolerable by the moment. Sensei offered a few cartons of cigarettes and American beer to Sifu, who smiled and accepted with a pleased response of appreciation. American cigarettes are hard to get, expensive, and much favored over the Eastern brands.

I came to find out later that Sifu uses them to barter trades and rent for the *dojo*. Whatever his needs were, American gifts were without a doubt a valuable commodity. In the final analysis, I couldn't decide whether his style was more Chinese or Japanese in nature. His students, if they were anything like the brown belt, were a team of fighting warriors.

We all exchanged goodbyes and I kept addresses in case the day came when I returned. After changing back to our street clothes, I breathed a sigh of relief upon my exit of this Philippine *gung fu dojo*. Sensei asked, "What are you thinking? Do you think you're going to make black belt some day?"

I fought not to show my pain and frustration setting in as the swelling in my rib cage continued to increase by the moment. I answered, "Without a doubt, Sensei, but my real concern is whether the *dojo* spider crawled into my shoe before I put it on!" Sensei smiled sarcastically, flagged down a taxi, and helped me into the seat. He knew without asking about the pain running through my body.

As I held on, the taxi flew through the backstreets, over and around mud holes, dodging pedestrians as they hung out and challenged our driver. The sun had set, and the nightlife with flashing neon glowed as we passed the bars and vendors attempting to lure money out of our pockets. Many nights would come over the next two or three weeks when I would spend the few military dollars I had in those bars.

A feeling of conquest ran through my veins as the humid wind blew through my service uniform and we sped to the base. Before our arrival, we stopped at the last night spot, the final watering hole, for a couple more beers. Holding my injuries as I exited the taxi, I stepped into a hole of muddy water and soaked my shoes once again. Sensei laughed. I looked down to see an advertisement flyer on the ground and picked it up. Discount drinks for military personnel, it read, no cover charge, two-drink and two-girl minimum. I was about to throw it away when some writing caught my eye. In penciled letters on the back I read the handwritten words: "Ten more days and I'm out of here—patience and perseverance to the end." I wondered how close the meaning was to my afternoon ordeal. At least the last part was. I knew whoever wrote it was soon to be discharged—homeward bound for the U.S. of A.

As we walked into the bar past the hustlers and bouncers I read a poster, "See the amazing Mona Lisa—46-22-36." I had to pay to get in. More stories and training yet to come, I thought. I supported myself on a stool next to the bar and yelled, "Please get me a Budweiser this time. No, make it three."

Shin—Heart

CHAPTER TWO

Battle beneath the Thunder

The 80,000-pound *USS Kittyhawk* cut its way through the dead-still Sea of Tonkin, south of the Asian continent off China. A new destination and secret operation had been set for a strike into the heart of North Viet Nam. The Da Nang Air Base was being used together with a large sea operation to flex muscles and express concerns for P.O.W.s without the usual diplomacy. This meant both day and night sea operations with flight ops continuing around the clock. We would be pounding the enemy's inland strongholds hard with heavy artillery, Napalm, and 500-pound bombs from the carrier strike force.

Recon flights had returned recently with photographs of North Viet Nam in preparation for a major thrust into the heart of enemy territory. Earlier in the week we had taken on heavy ordnance from a supply ship and refueled at sea. We carried out all specific tasks needed to steam our way to the proper site for operations. Prior to our launch date and time, bombs of all sizes were everywhere. Strung on the decks and lined up like tree trunks on carts, the heavy ordnance was being loaded on the fighters' wings both in the hangar bay and on the flight decks.

I took some time off from my shift in the master-at-arms division. Burning out was common at sea, without the feel of real land beneath your feet. Previous to my shift, I was directed to serve as a radarman, both operator and assistant's repairman. I had been living the life of a mole. I was buried deep within the ship in a darkened space. Here, all directions, speeds, and identities of aircraft and ship operations and hostile intruders were determined by the electronic sight of computers and radar communications.

Second-class or E-5 level was my present grade and offered me various opportunities for much freedom of movement and other privileges. My professional work also carried me into the Electronic Countermeasure division in CIC (Combat Information Center), where electronic frequency analysis became another of my duties.

Even with the added benefits of my new job, I was growing tired and needed rest and relaxation.

The typical grey steel color was everywhere as I made my way to the catwalk—a grid system with holes in the metal beneath your feet so water could pass through in heavy rain squalls and air could escape, drying the steel quickly. As I walked, I could see the sea raging below or calmly passing by, depending on the weather. Extending outward toward the distant sea, all was calm and visibility was endless. The hot, humid wind was thick as it blew up through the catwalk and made me feel as if I were walking on air. I walked down the catwalk as far as I could go, then jumped up on the flight deck at the front of the bow. I looked at the steel safety nets that hung out in front of the ship.

Things were relaxed between operations and I slid out on the steel net as far as I could and lay in the hot tropical sun to daydream. Looking down at the sea, I could watch the huge monster I was riding cut the salt water with its bow as the sea foam ran its hull and danced with the flying fish.

One wrong move and I would fall almost 100 feet into this snake-ridden jewel of the Orient. The wind at the front of the deck is powerful, and when opposing the direction of flight, creates extreme lift for the aircraft taking off. Although high above the water, I felt as though I were floating from time to time while my mind wandered in the frustration of a dreadful war. Two long years had passed and two more yet to go. One of my training buddies, Scot, arrived to do the same as I, and we both spoke of home and the next time we would arrive in port for R & R. We all were in hopes that Hong Kong would be our next port of entry with its bright lights, B-girls, and discount drinks. That was the scuttlebutt going around the ship, anyway.

We also heard that we could buy anything we wanted in Hong Kong or Japan at a fraction of what it cost stateside, so everyone would go on the beach rich from combat pay and come back on board broke.

Scot had been training with me for over six months now in Chinese *kempo* and was one of my best friends. He came from Boston and had all the East Coast accents and jive to go along with it. I, on the other hand, hailed from Motown, the Motor City, with the best black rock-and-roll. There were times I sounded like him and he like I in both manner and speech. It seemed we always had a laugh or joke to share. You just did whatever you could to get by the best way possible.

Scot was an intermediate green belt level fighter and I had just advanced to brown belt. He stood a good six-foot-one or -two, about 190 pounds, and was lean and quick. "Well, Jack," Scot said with a chuckle, "I hear Sensei is going to hold the 'Ruthless Iron Box' under the flight deck any day now and that you are one of the guys set to be in it." I groaned and rolled on my side sighing, "I know, I know."

"Yes, and Sensei said I need to pick a couple of green belts to go to the wall with me too, and it looks like you are going to be one of the four."

Scot went on, "I just did ten rounds yesterday and am sore as hell. No way."

I laughed, "Right, as if that makes a difference to me. I owe you a couple of shots anyway, Boston!"

The "Iron Box" was a seldom-used wrestling room under the flight deck forward, next to where the launch equipment and machinery were housed for catapults that jettisoned the fighters into the air during launching. Old wrestling mats covered the steel floor and others hung on some of the bulkheads in the small space used from time to time for falling and throws in *karate-do*. But worst of all, you couldn't hear because the vibration of the jets above was unbelievable. You couldn't breathe because the heat was unbearable. Temperatures during our cruise in the China Sea would soar above 100 degrees, and in the confines of this space the intense humidity would force the mercury to even higher levels.

Sensei used this area from time to time to test the fortitude of those who wanted to advance. During class, it was usually feared that your name would be called out for "iron box training." Each space on the ship (a name used for quarters where one slept or carried out a ship function) was contained by steel doors which swung shut and bolted together neatly to enforce watertight integrity in case of attack. General quarters for any nuclear or shipboard attack was practiced from time to time, so all doors were shut during these periods. Everyone suffered. I always wondered what type of world I would have to come back to in the event of such a cataclysm.

You couldn't leave or enter a space under most circumstances without jeopardizing the security of that particular space. You were confined for hours and sometimes days. The box was similar to the confined feeling of being trapped. Anyone who was forced to remain in the box had the space sealed during their practice, and Sensei had the sneaky way of surprising you from time to time to see if you met his demands. Flight operations would rage above, the air circulation was nil, and you would learn to endure.

This was a means to intensify our practice under adverse conditions. As for spaciousness, the iron box was twelve by twelve feet in size. Definitely not the Ramada Inn.

"At what time does special practice start, Jack?" Scot asked.

"About 5:00 PM, the same time as the first launch. I heard we will be in flight operations all night long, then a short morning break and back to it the rest of the day."

I lost track of time as my duties carried me into numerous shifts (both day and night) and the only thing that kept me sane was a movie on board or a special meal. Letters are the lifeline to one's inner mind. Without them, one grows weary and loses spirit. We all looked forward to mail call. For me, *karate* also served as a link to the real world as well as a mysterious Oriental counterpart. It was a means to clear the stale air which frequently finds its way to the core of one's existence. No matter how intense or demanding Sensei became, the time I spent was measured in new knowledge and personal development. It became a way out for many others as well. Scot and I shared these adventures many a time together.

I lay quietly allowing my thoughts to drift to a time and place that drew a smile across my dry lips. I picked a place and time back home, or an event with great friends with whom I grew up, and allowed the enjoyable details to consume my dreamland. Sea wind passed through my hair and over my face. I could hear the bow cut the open sea and sensed the power of the carrier beneath my body. I tried so hard to believe this was all a dream. Alas, I was unsuccessful and rudely awakened to reality. The dream world was wonderful, but reality hit hard when the loudspeaker sounded for operations to begin, and my ordeal as well. Now I would endure the next hour or two.

I wanted to lie here longer and rest my body. Scot shook my shoulder and mentioned, "Jack, you know how Sensei gets when you're late. Let's not piss him off."

I answered, "I know exactly, but my body says more rest." We both rose and walked back to our berthing space and picked up our uniforms. Earlier in the week, Sensei said he had a special surprise for us, so I had been seriously focusing on what it might be. I couldn't imagine what type of grueling exercise was planned but was sure it was a test of will. As it turned out, I would not be disappointed.

On the way to my quarters, I thought back to practice the other night when Sensei decided to drill the hell out of us with thousands of repetitions. We labored to hone our ability and learned to observe and check not only our physical movement, but our mental and spiritual acuity as well. Hammering our way through the ordeal of intensive class, we polished our weapons. Repetition is a great teacher in *karate*. It shows one the mistakes through intuitive study and, over time, one becomes proficient with great determination. With a sense of obsession one eventually becomes very efficient by mastering one's thinking and mental attitude.

As you become exhausted in practice, you find the inner strength to force yourself onward, one step at a time, and the resolution not to shrink from the challenges of life. That difficult class tested everyone's courage, and no one was allowed to leave lest they appear guilt-ridden at the next session.

It was one of those nights Sensei gave us unique insight into what we were attempting to accomplish. We came to understand that the Japanese have three treasures since ancient times representing the spirit of Japan. The three are the mirror, the sword, and the beads. Each stands for something different. Combined, they stand for wisdom, benevolence, and courage—the three great treasures within our lower stomach, called the *hara*. It is said that if one focuses on this area and trains with all his soul, it will lead to enlightenment and the awakening of the mind. It is the spiritual significance of hard practice and relentless training that keeps one from the violent use of his martial art. This is what intense practice led me to believe.

Scot and I grabbed our uniforms and headed for the Iron Box. Moving from space to space through the passageways, I felt as though I were traveling a catacomb in an ancient land, forced to meet my opponent and do battle at the end in some type of dueling arena. Flight operations started, and as we got closer to the training location, the sound of fighters, arresting gear, and launching catapults grew increasingly louder. North Viet Nam would feel the wrath of the U.S. Navy this night.

It was a strange feeling. I was going to do battle in this huge ship floating on the South China Sea. Above, the same action was taking place on a different scale. The ship shook with each launch only several feet above my head where rubber wheels and jet engine blasts met steel. Finally arriving at the space, I saw that the watertight door was shut and a note remained fixed to the handle. Removing it I read, "Take the ankle weights, place them on your feet, and tape them securely in place. Take the old padded life jackets, put them on, and secure them with tape so they don't come loose during battle, allowing you an excuse to stop." A large wooden box next to the hatch contained everything I hoped not to find. The tools and rules were there, but still, what was next? We looked at one another with concern.

There we stood like robots, secretly wondering if Sensei's mind was in order. I had about ten pounds of weight braced to my ankles, and then another ten strapped to my body. The old vest had to be taped to my ribs and shoulders, so movement was hindered at first. I knew vaguely that I would be abused in some ancient fashion which

I had not yet experienced. I wondered what test of endurance, patience, and skill Sensei himself had to be subjected to during his junior years when first starting *karate* in Hawaii.

Already sweating and waiting for orders, I heard distant voices coming down the passageway. To my astonishment, two more warriors were coming wearing the same strange outfits. Arriving, they looked at us amused as though we were something out of a futuristic science fiction movie. Scot and I studied the other two students, who were no strangers, as both men were advanced technicians. One of the two, Angelo, gave us the blueprint of what was to become of us. He said, "Gentlemen, our training is as follows: one hour in the box, resistance combat or *kotekitei*." That was it. We would match off, and one person would attack the other until we dropped. The idea was to serve as a punching bag, a standing target who would be pummeled to death. We could counterattack to launch anything from our arsenals possible, but I knew it would be improbable to offer the speed and tactics I normally administered with all the weight I had to bear.

Creating the strength to withstand punishment was Sensei's highest goal for as long as I knew him. We learned to resist and blend. He used to say that "in order to understand the warfare strategy of attacking, one must be attacked and learn to harness, redirect, and harmonize the opponent's force and *ki*."

We were screaming at the top of our lungs attempting to communicate while the flight ops continued. Flipping a coin, I got Angelo, who was definitely not my first choice. Here I was, 135 pounds, against a brute of 180 who said little and thought in terms of a wrecking machine. We all agreed that it was time to begin our ordeal. Opening the watertight hatch, which was half the size of a normal entrance way, we slipped through one at a time. The heat rushed out of the darkness, surprising us with a familiar sound like that of opening a coffee can. The hatch swung open as a powerful draft of heat hit us in the face like a blast from a furnace. The temperature was at least 110 degrees. The air was so hot, I could feel it as it passed through my throat down into my lungs. One of the other boys groped in the half-darkness for the light switch, then found it. Flipping it on, the rust-colored and grey bulkheads reflected the bizarre conditions we would face. Condensation ran down each surface from the elements, and the steel floor was equally as disturbing. Now barefoot, my feet turned black from the grime and grease of the space where we would do battle. *What have I subjected myself to in the name of honor?* I contemplated. Quite the reverse of the streamlined, glitzy *dojos* of today.

I reflected back to old Japan and the special practice known as *Shochugeiko no Hachigatsu,* or summer outdoor training, in August. This was the hottest time of year in the southern Japanese islands. Under the relentless heat of the August sun, crops grew well and flourished, but in the marshy bogs of the countryside, hordes of mosquitoes bred just as rapidly, making constant forays to the human blood supply nearby. With the heat, the blood-sucking pests made August most miserable for the feudal Japanese *samurai* and every class, from peasant to emperor.

Japanese referred to these kinds of days as *mushiatsui,* extremely muggy. To defend against the unbearable heat, both the country and city dwellers relied upon the cleverly designed *sudare* (bamboo strip blinds). Japanese homes of the times were surrounded by *fusuma* (solid screens built of soft wood and rice paper). Most of the year, *fusuma,* as did *shoji* (sliding screens), offered protection against the elements, but in August, nothing could restrain the attack of the most frustrating weather. One alternative that the *Nihonjin* used was a concoction of chrysanthemum flowers mixed in with specially made incense. When burned, this potion served to repel the mosquitoes.

The blend was burned in small handmade pot-belly pig figurines. Inside the pots, the incense burned while the smoke and the fragrance drifted through the statues' nostrils and mouths. It seemed everyone used the decoration, as they were found everywhere and people moved within their homes as if walking in a thick morning fog.

It was during this time that the *samurai* gathered for austerity training, or *shugyo.* For a period of three days, warriors from different regions would partake in the extremely intense *shugyo* to find their awakening through exhaustive and continuous dueling. It was obvious that

outdoors, there was no protection from the elements except the continuous motion of battle. Those who survived the ritual to be victorious were few. But these became legends of the time due to their
prowess in the fierce competition. *Samurai* from all over the region
would compete in this annual summer martial arts festival. Many, it
was said, came away injured and crippled for life. But thus was war,
and the obvious goals that drove those who fought onward: honor
and enlightenment.

Today in distant martial communities this traditional ritual still
exists. Once *samurai* dealt in this practice of conflict. Now it is the
empty-hand practitioners of *karate, judo,* and *jujitsu* that keep this
ancient tradition alive. In circles of *Budoka,* this is known as *kogangeiko,*
or exchange of courtesies practice. The competition began with courtesy, a highly respected virtue of the martial artist, but as patience
wore thin and frustration broke through, courtesy usually gave way
to anger.

Those seeking an understanding of their skill and mental powers
would meet in this three-day event to fight and duel to the end. All
those who entered on all levels of proficiency knew not what type or
level of opponent stood in front of them because all wore only the
white belt. No one knew the other's rank, or he would be influenced
and intimidated from the outset.

It was common for black belts to find themselves pitted against a
white belt who was aggressive but inexperienced or against a seasoned
technician who used the cunning skill found after twenty-five or
thirty-five years of practice on the hard wooden floors or *tatami.* Three
days of the most intense weather, infested with the worst insects, and
against the greatest of odds. One fought the emotions against the current of the tides, and strove to win the honors of purification and
community recognition. One would think that all of Nihon (Japan)
was composed of great warriors, but life's not that generous, and few
exceptional *Budoka* existed. Thoughts of timeworn tradition and
ancient Japan flowed through my veins. The ritual of dueling was
presently upon me.

We paired off that day in 'Nam, and gained a deeper understanding of the ultimate challenge and human resistance found only in the mortal heat of battle. Our spirits soared and we fought relentlessly hard, "steadfast like a mountain." Facing Angelo—who threw me from steel wall to steel wall—was very difficult and fearful, to say the least. After fifteen minutes my feet felt like they were anchored in concrete. My legs began to shake, cramp, and worse yet, give out. Now, instead of countering attacks, I only hung on to offer resistance and endure the blitz that Angelo leveled at me. My head spun, and I could hear Scot against the wall beside me groaning with pain.

Time dragged by and Angelo shouted at me to counter, but I had little resistance left to continue the struggle. Still, I covered my vulnerable areas and slipped as many kicks or punches driven into me. My mind became a compulsive entity with a single goal of withstanding the attack. From time to time, I would collide with Scot on the wall beside me as he fought and stumbled in my direction. Our *keikogi* were stained from the rust-colored paint.

The protection I wore seemed to offer a buffer between my chest and his blows, but the shock of me between his fists and the wall grew increasingly unforgiving. I now found myself stuck in place and my legs could no longer bear the pain of dodging. The cramping would soon set in, bringing me to my knees unless time or Angelo were finished.

I also noticed that Angelo was growing weary and that his attacks were now becoming weak by the very enemy we all fear, the decline of emotional and physical conditioning, which leads to failure. I slid further down the steel wall into a corner of the space where bulkhead met bulkhead. I could see Scot out the corner of my eye now on the floor with his adversary standing over him sucking wind. His battle was over. The walls shook and vibrated as the big birds relentlessly launched into the skies above. I noticed Angelo now beginning to falter, which served to give me confidence. My wits somehow became sharper and in some way reignited as though I were on full autopilot.

A series of kicks came in again, striking my chest gear and rattling my brain momentarily, but I stood my ground. I felt as if I were holding up the Great Wall of China. I knew he was trying to beat me into submission, but that I would not tolerate. Soaking wet with sweat and covered in grime, we ground our teeth and fought on.

He backed off and yelled for me to counter once again, taunting me with his challenging words, then in a moment lunged in full power with a driving front kick to my lower midsection. At the last instant I leaned aggressively out of the way, thrusting my body to the left as his foot missed the mark and collided with the steel wall. I heard the bang and the crunch. Down he went twisting in pain. I reached over to help him up, but it was too overbearing for me, as I was totally exhausted, too jaded from battle, and it was too painful for him to stand.

The door to the space flew open, and there stood Sensei.

"It looks as if I'm too late for practice, men!" He stepped in the room, looking frustrated with us, and helped Angelo up and out the door. The rest of us feebly crawled through the hatch after him in fear we would be left to continue. I fell to the deck gasping for fresh air, as did Scot and his partner. As we rested, the attack wing continued to launch above us in full force, relentless in their task. I ran my hands over the cool deck under my feet and leaned on the air-conditioned wall in the passageway.

We would later learn that Angelo had broken his ankle. Thinking of the battle, I realized that not once had I gotten a full blow in. But then I did get a valuable lesson I remembered from a hangar bay encounter some time ago. "Use nature to defeat your enemy and practice side moves." At that point, I held firm the resolve to practice movement until I couldn't be touched in battle. It wasn't until later in my training while back in Michigan that I realized the total importance of dodging on a systematic level. Tactics and timing were the keys to survival. We all lay there motionless until we could regain our composure and come back to our normal senses. Sitting in a daze, I thought how I used this personal abuse to forget the war and the pain of missing home. Aside from the Zen battles I faced day to day, all I had were my memories of buddies back home and my family.

I heard footsteps, and raising my head I noticed a small group of Marines coming down the passageway. As they passed by, they recognized us as the crazy *karate* boys known on board for our cruel physical testing of human endurance. As they stepped over our bodies stretched across the aisle, one sarcastically blurted out, "Boot camp." I responded, "We have class tomorrow at six, boys." They drifted out of view and acknowledged me with only a glance. I slowly stripped away my contact gear, peeled off my weights, and then heard Sensei say, "I'm holding class in this space tomorrow, so be on time."

I answered, "Yes, Sensei, I'll be there," as did the others, except for Angelo who still remained in distress.

I really couldn't imagine the brutality of going through an hour of practice, let alone fifteen minutes. We all stood up at last and helped Angelo to sick bay for whatever steps were needed to repair his ankle. I thought he was going to pay me hell the next time we fought, but supporting him down the passageway he looked over to me and said, "Good move, Jack."

I responded, "Thanks Angelo," and caught a smile. We were fairly good friends after that.

Struggling for strength to get back to work at the master-at-arms division, the memory of my previous battle played itself out in my mind. Stepping out of a watertight door, I stood high above the hangar stretching out in front of me. It looked like a maze of city lights and bustling activity with war planes everywhere. I made my way through, thinking of the sweating steel walls in the Iron Box, the intensity of the humid heat, and the crashing sound of the war machine grinding its jet engines overhead, all of which served to hone my skill even more.

I learned to focus and cultivate the *seishin tanren,* forge of the spirit. I gained a deeper realization and distinct understanding of combining and utilizing basic skills, footwork, and tactics. The *maai,* or combative engagement distance, a point at which the opponent is close enough to correctly strike or be struck, was a crystal-clear benchmark in my newfound struggle to excellence. I had much yet to learn. I now came to understand the true purpose of what I was doing, that the battle itself wasn't the real point of all this, only a means to master my perceptions of the *Budo* way. The ultimate understanding in my practice was to clearly define and master the forging of my spirit.

I felt how my body had become united in its purpose at specific points in the battle. It was truly a distinguishable fact that physical mechanics and theory must be integrated as one, united by the spirit in the heat of practice throughout one's entire life. "These understandings can only be found in real battle, not theory." I wanted more as I became obsessed to find the truth in those fleeting experiences where light momentarily found darkness.

Arriving back at my division, I immediately fell to the deck exhausted, and directed my gaze at Sensei sitting at a desk. He told me, "Jack, you are closing in on the truth and you're going to be the best. Just give it time, give it time. Be like the bamboo, bend with the elements and spring back with life." I answered, "I will do my best, Sensei."

Flight operations had ceased and I hadn't even noticed that the war had fallen silent. Only my recent battle remained in my mind. I hit the showers and allowed the "cold" water to run down my face. In the tropics, the water is always warm or hot, never cold as we know it. Leaning my shoulder against the stainless steel shower wall, I was exhausted. I felt my bruises, my superficial injuries. Thinking of my battle and the promise of class the next day in the Iron Box, I said aloud, "Tomorrow is a good day to die."

I drifted into Zen momentarily, where peace prevails and the world remains silent as a night in the deepest forest. Learning to find my "way" was becoming manifest.

Avoid Promotion While Young

To be promoted and serve as a useful *samurai* while still young cannot bear fruitful results; however bright by nature, the young man's ability is not yet ripe enough to convince others. It is better, therefore, to start coming into one's own gradually at the age of fifty or thereabout. A man whose promotion has appeared too slow for his ability in others' eyes can effectively obtain truly favorable results in his service.

Also, a man who has dissipated his fortune but kept up his noble causes can soon recover from such a spot because of the absence of cravings for selfish gain.

—from the *Hagakure*

Toh Kon——Fighting Spirit

CHAPTER THREE

Yokusuka Shotokan

Flying air strike sorties off the coast of 'Nam came to an abrupt end one hot summer night in 1967. The carrier fleet had been at sea fifty long days and everyone was ready for a positive break and R & R. Being informed that our destination would be either Japan or Hong Kong led to a great enthusiastic uplift for us all. Japan was usually our last stop en route to the States after an overseas tour of duty had been completed. This return was usually for repairs or overhaul, hence mutiny could be expected from every human being on board. At any rate, soon after the word was out: Nihon it was, and so our long trek to the far-off Japanese Pearl began.

Sensei Love had mentioned to me that over the next two weeks while en route we would be involved in intense practice, as he expected to go to a *dojo* in Yokusuka that he once visited. This was a *Shotokan dojo* which followed the traditional teachings of Funakoshi Sensei, known as the father of Japanese *karate-do*. Funakoshi Sensei introduced his style of martial arts in 1923 after leaving the Ryukyu Islands (Okinawan Islands). I am able to present some information in retrospect on the *Shotokan* style. *Shotokan* is known as a hard-style form. In almost every *Shotokan dojo* in *Nihon* are the words written by Gichin Funakoshi Sensei: "The ultimate aim of the art of *karate-do* lies not in victory or defeat, but in the perfection of the character of its participants." Actually, *karate* was initially called *tode* (Chinese hand), then later Funakoshi Sensei changed the first character of the word to mean "empty" and thus *karate* became known as "empty

51

hand" rather than "Chinese hand."

Like Chinese *kempo,* Japanese *kenpo,* or a range of other forms of *Budo,* martial arts has a defined ideology of identity and purpose. I was beginning to seek out higher discernment as well as increased mastery. As experience paid off, I found that physical hardships were necessary to excel, but spiritual practice is necessary for perfecting physical skill. It was therefore much easier to understand later on that a martial artist advances not only in his or her physical abilities, but also his or her holistic comprehension and development. I became wiser with time and greatly interested in as many *karate dojo*s as I could find, whether in the Orient or stateside. This gave me greater insight and a means to gauge my personal growth in the big picture. By having access to many *dojo*s I gained a great prize in which my knowledge could improve to unbelievable levels.

Sensei gave me some of his notes and books to brush up on some of the knowledge from other systems I would come in contact with on each visit to various *dojo*s during my overseas duty. Over time I collected quite a good library. I knew Sensei's knowledge was limited because of the vast confusion and rivalry among differing styles and systems. Knowledge is power. Reading, I found a quote from Funakoshi Sensei:

> Just as an empty valley can carry a resounding voice, so must the person who follows the Way of *Karate* make himself void or empty by ridding himself of all self-centeredness and greed. Make yourself empty within, but upright without. This is the real meaning of the 'empty' in *karate. Karate* alone explicitly states the basis of all martial arts. Form equals emptiness—emptiness equals form. The use of the character in *karate* is indeed based on this principle.

It should be pointed out that the word *Budo* or "martial arts" literally translates as "the Way of Stopping Conflict." This word is distinctly drawn from its counterpart *Bujutsu,* meaning "military science" or "war art." *Karate* presently is referred to in Japan by many as *karate-do* and is understood to be much more than a fighting system. Funakoshi

Sensei claimed that *karate-do* promotes and cultivates a spiritual and philosophical foundation for the *karate* technician in his practice. Thus many of the Japanese martial arts were transformed from a fighting art into an art or discipline of the Way, a discipline leading to self-development and enlightenment which through time found its place among the distinct Japanese *Budo* systems.

The knowledge gained by one's experience in martial arts becomes knowledge that serves as a guide to a higher level of personal understanding and enhanced consciousness. Confusion and conflict lead to mental frustration and self-defeat. Higher learning allows the sun to find the break in the clouds to burn through and enlighten. One learns to exemplify the highest standards of the traditional *Budo* only if one continually surpasses even his own expectations.

I knew the course I chose would be one of great adversity accompanied by the constant injury one encounters while shaping an indomitable spirit. In the Japanese tradition, this is termed *seishin tanren* or spirit-forging—to forge a strong spirit.

As our ship headed toward Japan, I immediately undertook a diligent training regimen in preparation for the next *dojo* I was to discover under the guidance of my teacher. I was told that the *dojo* in mind would either allow us to train or limit us to watch. Many Japanese *dojo senseis* have a policy which does not permit any outsiders to share in the action unless they wear a white belt and make entrance for the consideration of acceptance into that particular *dojo*. I knew that whatever happened, it would bring new knowledge and excitement into my life.

Each day I started doing road work or, I should say, *deck* work, by running the flight deck at dawn. My special practice was observed and guided by Sensei. I watched my diet closely and ate great amounts of California jackrabbit and eggs supplied by the ship's kitchen.

One training practice included climbing our divisional radar tower. This enclosed monstrosity on the ship was set up similar to a square silo with ten levels. When you looked up the ladder, it didn't look very high, but after your third or fourth climb, coming down became a chore as your arms burned to hold you from falling. This would prove important in my later training, with the role of *kata tetore* or wrist-grabbing in the art of *aikijitsu*. My arms strengthened over the weeks that followed, my chest became more defined, and my *kumite* (free-sparring) improved dramatically.

Each evening during sunset, I took a calm stroll to the fantail of the ship and after meditation at dusk, performed *kata* (forms) training as instructed. Sensei would accompany me in the manner of the workouts he planned during our steam to Yokusuka, Japan. As I walked to the fantail one late afternoon through the hangar bay—the common route for various destinations on the ship—the hangar was quiet as I gazed from war plane to war plane. Most of the lights were at half power, so the the war had somehow become silent. Only the cadence of the surf smashing into the hull could be heard as the ship cut through the sea heading north.

I had recently encountered another shipmate in a disagreement over male macho dominance which I felt was foolishly handled and shrugged it off. On the other hand, my borderline counterpart was outraged that I had so calmly made him appear to look like an idiot during our confrontation. I remember him warning me that no matter what type of *karate* I knew, I had better watch my back. Fighting or any type of misconduct was frowned upon, with straight brig time followed by abusive labor with the Marines as watchdogs and guards. The humiliation one had to endure was the worst, to say the least. I knew I wanted shore leave and not a foolish court martial.

Stepping under the wings of the A-1 jets or the F-4 Phantoms was nothing out of the ordinary; I walked this way every day to the mess hall. I moved forward quickly. The air in the hangar was dry and cool now that we were steaming ahead in open sea, but a presence hung in the midst of it and I could not shake an uneasy feeling. The lights in the bay went off and on, then flickered and remained at half power—most likely being corrected for an electrical malfunction. The smell of aviation gasoline was everywhere, as were the missiles, many of which hung in place from the bottom of the fighter wings. Passing one of the aircraft, I noticed a six-inch hole in the port wing. Strange as it may seem, many of the surface-to-air missiles (SAMS) launched at the aircraft do not detonate on impact. This pilot and plane, it seemed, were lucky—the missile passed through the wing without exploding. I was sure this was the stuff of stories many pilots never forget.

I noticed a couple of other sailors moving down the hangar in the same direction as I, but could only catch a glimpse of their legs as they walked behind the other aircraft hidden from clear view. No doubt on their way to chow, moving the same direction on the other side of the hangar bay. Approaching the last plane, one of the larger recon aircraft, I rounded the corner to come face to face with my most recent problem. Same big mouth; we'll call him "Tom." I stopped and glared at him and his buddy for a brief moment. Standing next to the aircraft with my back to the side of the fuselage, I held my ground. I had a queasy feeling inside like a battle of wits, or that flesh would meet flesh in the next few moments. His partner seemed to back him up and position himself to the side of me momentarily as I shuffled closer to the side of the aircraft so as to cover my back. Lying to his outside were several 100-pound bombs on a bomb rack carrier resting on the steel hangar bay deck. I tried to remain calm and show little emotion, but inside I felt the wave of adrenaline beginning to intensify. Emotion can become your worst enemy when faced with mortal danger.

"Well, if it isn't Mr. Kara*hhh*te!" He didn't even finish the breath of his last word when a looping roundhouse haymaker sailed through the air toward my face. Stepping the opposite direction in a ducking-type motion, I swiftly kicked his inner thigh with my instep, full power. I knew the top of my foot found its mark from the look that crossed his face. In the same instant, he buckled as his roundhouse punch faltered, losing its steam. To my glorious surprise, his fist collided with the side of the plane and surely must have broken. As he grabbed his knuckles in pain, the slow-motion momentum of his body falling carried him over the bomb cart on the deck and down he went. His buddy was nowhere to be found. If I recall, as Tom punched, his buddy flew in the opposing direction.

I looked at him confidently and strode off. Fortunately, no Marines were present or anyone else to confirm or dispute what took place. I had a story to tell Sensei, but more importantly, I learned a useful lesson: "Use nature to your own advantage." Learn to blend and apply more significant practice in qualified movement, and use dodging in abundance.

On a side deck adjacent to the hangar bay was an area where you could practice while the ship cut through the surf and the wind blew through your hair. The appearance of the flight deck hanging over your head about fifty feet above, combined with the power of the aircraft carrier moving forward, created an odd illusion and a worthy freak of nature. It was there that I would begin my practice of dodging and counterattacking with the rhythm of the wind and the spray of salt water at each huge wave deflected off the hull. I found a realization in my battle that afternoon, and learned that reflection on victory or defeat is an immediate consideration. If one does not take steps to understand the self in the midst of enlightenment, then enlightenment will quickly lose its definition and significance. It was important that I now become more focused on my goals and adjust to my needs. I kept telling myself to absorb what was useful and discard what was not. I knew that training had to become intensified to maximum proportions if I were to gain the mindset familiar only to the masters of the days of old.

Sensei had mentioned that practice and training were to be constant and without reserve. I found out that the true essence of *Budo* actually occurs when one can transcend any and all conflict, to free oneself from the mental bonds of restraint—to grow and transform all fears into spiritual achievement. To know my mind was one of my goals, but first I had to harness a sound ability to perform under all pressures.

As I stood at the front of the line in the mess hall, I reached for a tray. Sensei noticed me and waved to me to join him for dinner. Two other master-at-arms petty officers were sitting with him at the table. I picked my meal and walked over to the boys. We greeted each other with the typical swabby language and sarcastically exchanged looks. We quickly consumed our meals and it was not long before the other two swabbies left for their patrol to secure various areas of the ship.

I reached for my coffee, which was so hot it burned me. I found it almost impossible to hold the cup. Sensei asked me why I was so shaky. "What happened, Jack? Tell me the untold news." Either Sensei's martial arts intuition had told him exactly what occurred or someone ran down to the mess hall who witnessed the encounter and mentioned it to him. I found out over the years that a *sensei* has the unique ability to sense specific things before they actually happen. This may explain why he knew that something had occurred before my arrival.

"In old martial arts systems the experience that a practitioner gained was found to be the ultimate teacher; experience breeds self-enlightenment. Students were taught in a nonverbal, highly intuitive manner of learning. Over long years one finds more than a purely physical understanding of things as the spiritual intuition influences one's whole life in a manner that applies to all things."

"Jack, you're not very calm right now, I can sense it." I opened up to Sensei and explained the whole situation as it unfolded in the last thirty minutes or so. I thought Sensei would be disgruntled by my actions, but he smiled and told me to write down something of importance. I reached for my pen and the chit-pad that all master-at-arms carry with them. I wrote:

"Watch the eyes, they are the mirrors to the souls. Watch the head, it shows movement and emotion. Watch the mind, it can find victory or defeat. Watch the void, for it is nothing—and one's mind must become nothingness, it must become empty."

Sensei went on to say, "Take the side move you did and practice tonight, late on the flight deck in the dark, just the one movement, and perform it 2,000 times, then meditate for three or four minutes, go to bed, and visualize the same movement in your mind thirty times or until you sleep. Do you understand, Jack?"

"Yes, Sensei, I do." I knew that this meant fixing in my mind as well as my physical body the right action needed for specific responses to attacks. So I consumed myself with the task of repeating the move that most likely saved my face and head. I also slept soundly that magnificent night, sure of my victory even though my opponent had weighed a hearty 210 pounds. Pride ran through my veins knowing I weighed only 135 pounds.

Over the weeks during our transit, maximum training practices played themselves out. The focus on the ship became one of anticipation of our arrival on shore. All of the ship's company were required to perform distinct duties that entailed cleaning up and buffing the entire aircraft carrier and its fighter wing prior to our arrival in Yokusuka. Training practice was becoming more intense as Sensei pushed me hard in my *kumite* (free-sparring). Our next outing in the streets of Oriental philosophy and Buddhism grew closer. Students were dead-set in their ways, either cultivating an invincible character or dropping out. Seeing students come and go was a common occurrence, as the discipline to follow through was one of determination in the pain department.

Practice lasted into the night as the makeshift *dojo*'s steel walls developed condensation. It would run down to the deck and create a slippery surface we had to deal with if we planned to finish the class. My 135-pound body knew the harsh reality of continual focus and repetition needed to build endurance and master application.

The limited mats we used felt the successive pounding of bodies with as many as thirty students moving like waves of fish as we were thrown one body after another and hammered into the deck of enlightenment. *Kiai*s echoed down the long corridors of that section of the ship. It seemed that a supernatural entity filled the atmosphere for two or three hours.

I knew something special had been placed before me, so as other sailors and Marines took to the movie theaters or recreation halls to relax between the unreasonable conflicts of the Viet Nam War, I stood like a rock, striking the sand-filled pad on the steel beam, hardening my elbows and knuckles in a hypnotic state, conquering my difficult destiny. With each strike, the thud of my elbow sent vibrations down my spine and into the deck below. Sailors laughed and played cards in the next space down the corridor and I was sure frustrated by the noise, but I continued striking and no one interfered. I became obsessed with my daily ordeals and found great harmony in the workouts that lay before me with each new sun. It was a matter of dealing with immediate adversity to gain future proficiency. I polished the Way morning and night, never allowing my mind to weaken under my mission even though others fell by the wayside or diminished in their tasks. The sword began to take on a luster found only through my hardship. I had found the martial arts and it had consumed me. I knew then that I would become a black belt someday.

I felt like the *samurai* of old. In those times, a *samurai* would take to the streets on a pilgrimage. This journey led to the continual mastery of sword and mind, or *mushashugyo*. While traveling, these *samurai* honed their skills by challenging other masters in the martial art of swordsmanship, not always in a life-and-death struggle. As one can imagine, however, jealousy could cause heated tempers and mistakes which often led to a grim end. It seemed I was on a similar pilgrimage.

At last, only three hours remained before our battle carrier entered the port of Yokusuka. I met with Sensei for morning coffee on the catwalk and spoke of training practice and other students who seemed dedicated in their *karate* discipline. "Jack, I feel we now have a small loyal nucleus that will be with the ship over the next few years. I need to plan a brown belt and black belt test soon. You know, you have been practicing three to six hours daily, seven days per week, and I am going to recommend your test soon. Most people on the beach [the mainland] seem to think two sessions per week are good enough, but I believe you found out why training each day must become your own personal way. It must consume your very essence."

We spoke a long time about *karate* and it seemed Sensei always gave me insight from encounters of past battles and his demanding accomplishments. *Karate* was his mainstay. I could see it in his movement, his speech, and his manner.

I stared at the horizon toward the Japanese Islands with a new awareness that *karate* must become a "supreme expression of beautiful violence." My thoughts became a philosophy and my philosophy became action. Backed by obvious results, I could see my dreams materialize in a shape that excited the very essence of my obsession.

I had to train more. I had to supersede my own expectations to achieve the highest vigilance attainable. The moment and the challenge to come were all that remained in an ever-growing quest to face the enemy and find true honor based on victory.

Arriving once again in Nippon, excitement stimulated my spirit with the anticipation of adventure and advanced martial arts knowledge soon to be discovered in another *dojo*. The beautiful islands of the Japans, as it was called, were a maze of sharp, jagged, low mountains landscaped by thick pine trees and a precious variety of natural wonder. The small towns were clean and thriving with commerce. Yokusuka was a port city and to a large extent, a military town. Our arrival into the city was eagerly awaited, as I was anxious to find out what was in store for me on this leg of my journey along my Way.

Liberty call came immediately, and since I didn't pull any shore or ship duty, both Sensei and I were free to spend the next eight days on tour of the local area. As the Navy was his career, Sensei knew where to go and where not to go from all his previous experience over the years. As usual, I felt extremely comfortable and secure with the wrecking machine next to me in any situation.

With our uniforms pressed and clean, we both took our liberty in town, finding panhandlers and hustlers in an area called Thieves Alley. This was the mercantile and nightlife district sectioned off for everyone who wished to spend their ship's pay saved while at sea. During the morning and afternoon, various types of military personnel flooded into the streets on shopping sprees. At night the journeys often ended in drinking contests. It seemed like an exodus as an entire aircraft carrier and its destroyer escorts emptied all their personnel for a week on the town. The merchants, bar girls, and bar owners all relished the abundant income they would receive.

We jumped out of the cab at the edge of town, which was an experience in itself with a *kamikaze* driver, and began to walk the main street in pursuit of a few gifts to send back home to our loved ones and friends. These moments of finding new Oriental treasures were in a way sad, because of the graphic reminder of the great distance between me and my loved ones, home, and memories. It would be an entire year before I could take my leave and return to Michigan for a mere two weeks' vacation, then shortly afterward my permanent separation from the U.S. Navy. These few days out of each year were short compared to the four long years I was enduring in my tour of duty, primarily spent in the vicinity of the 'Nam crisis. Mixed emotions and frustration had to be dealt with during these periods in my life. It was without question a Catch-22. *Karate* saved me.

I honored Sensei's presence and his guidance on the Japanese people and ways as the day drifted by with little mentionable disorder. That same evening we bar-hopped for a brief period without allowing ourselves to get too intoxicated.

The next morning found us in a cab heading for a *dojo* located outside Yokusuka for an introduction to Japanese *Shotokan karate.* The outskirts of town were rural and set in orderly fashion. In fact, I noticed that everything was more organized and without the mayhem common to the Philippines. Honorable greetings and customary bows of respect were found with every individual I encountered. Traditionalism bound by rich customs was ingrained into the populace throughout Japan as a part of their nature. Something very special was happening to me as the days rolled by and I became more intrigued by these Oriental counterparts and their ways.

Approaching the outskirts of town, Sensei asked the cab driver to pull over and let us out. A gust of hot morning westerly wind blew at my face, no doubt a sign that the great *Budo* was ever-present. I looked around and noticed the approaching noonday sun reflecting down the street, glittering off the windows of the many traditional Japanese houses lined in neat rows. Here it seemed the pace was much slower as people passed by wearing the traditional *yukata kimono* and *geta.* The *geta,* or wooden shoes, made a clunking noise as they struck the brick and concrete. Here we found the people more connected to the earth, as more were farmers and merchants of the indigenous manner set upon surviving in their specific trades.

The rooftops were made of Japanese clay tiles and resembled the Oriental roofs seen earlier in Hong Kong. These same tiles were used in *tameshiwari* techniques in traditional *dojo*s by *karate-do* practitioners to test the strength and spirit of the striking power common to *Budo*—the martial way. Sensei had mentioned this to me during one of our long discussions of *Budo* in the Orient. It was not long before I would witness many of the things spoken of by Sensei at sea.

On the way to the *dojo,* Sensei stopped at a custom tailor shop and began to exchange information with the owner when I noticed him picking out several different bolts of material held on racks. I realized that Sensei was having a couple of quality suits made for him over the next few days, then he also instructed the owner, named Yuji, to prepare a man's *kimono* for me. For the next hour or so, we were measured and fitted by a few of Yuji's shop employees who stuck us with needles and pins attempting to get the most accurate fit possible. I did not quite know if this was some primitive form of acupuncture or if we were just human pin cushions. They seem to enjoy the action and laughed as they went on with their tasks. Each time one of the girls finished her job, a polite bow would follow with a genuine humble response of appreciation. Some of the finest silks and threads in the world, or so I assumed, lined the walls and hung from the ceiling. I found some new mystery at every turn in this magical place.

Soon we finished, paid the proper deposit, and off we strode like two *samurai* in a merchant's festival. Sensei said, "Jack, stop here. The *dojo* is around the corner and I met this old *sensei* once before, so do as I do and follow my every movement. Today is supposed to be a private demonstration in the traditional manner held for the annual anniversary of the *dojo.* Do you understand?"

"Yes, Sensei," I said.

"No, from now on say *hai,* Sensei or *ie,* which means 'yes' or 'no.'" I came to attention stance and bowed. "*Hai,* Sensei," I said.

We stepped around the corner and faced a short dead-end street with small houses connected on each side. The street was busy with merchants displaying vegetables and various other goods. Everyone you approached wanted you to spend some *okane* (money) before you passed them, but I was never harassed or panhandled by strangers. The two-story cramped buildings were neatly packed together with doors called *shoji* which slid sideways to allow one to enter and the sun or light to do the same. At the end of the street was a large *shoji* door opened fully, above three larger steps. No doubt the entrance to the *dojo*. In bold print above the *shoji* were Japanese characters called *moji* inscribed in wood. They meant *karate-do*. We removed our shoes and placed them on the large entrance deck to the *dojo* along with the many others which were organized into fine order. As we entered the *idiguchi* (doorway), eyes fixed themselves on us for a moment then faded away. *Gaijin* or foreigners were welcome, but not too openly. All the students were lined up on one side of the *dojo* in several rows, while senior instructors assisted in ritualistic *tameshiwari* and exhibition with the chief instructor. The *dojo* was extremely packed and unfortunately quite hot and humid.

A junior instructor *(kohai)* came over to us in the formal *samurai* approach. This walk seemed strange because he did so on his knees. All the students were in the formal seated position in perfect order, listening and watching the chief *sensei* explain his philosophy on *karate-do*. We were instructed to move to the rear corner and sit the same way and observe. The *dojo* had been built high off the ground and the floors were all covered with traditional *tatami* mats made of pressed reeds. These mats had a wonderful smell and were three feet by six feet in size, fitted together perfectly to form a unique floor on which to practice. The ceiling was high, made of natural colors, and beams made of light-colored polished wood spanned the length of the room from all sides.

In the front of the *taijo* (training area) was a shrine, or *jinja,* fitted into an alcove *(tokonoma).* Within it hung more *kanji* on a hand-painted scroll which looked familiar but my interpretation was undoubtedly wrong. The *kanji* and *sumi-e* were bordered by two ancient candle holders that stood reverently on either side. Later Sensei mentioned to me that the words meant *Budo.* There in the center, I became aware of simplicity and peace. A very small vase with a Japanese flower arrangement sat beside the *kanji.* At the front of the *dojo* (which was called the *shomen)* was a photo high on the wall of Gichin Funakoshi, father of modern-day *karate*. The founder of

Shotokan karate-do held vigilance over his students, teachers, and warriors of old. This was the man to whom they paid honor and respect for his original work.

To my right on the wall hung a rack designed to hold the Japanese sword, or *Nippon-to,* as it was called. The horizontal racks are called *katana-kake* even if they are not used to display swords at all. There, several *boken* (wooden swords) were arranged in an order up and down the rack in various sizes. I assumed they were used for defense against sword and club attacks and I found out later that I was right. Not only were they a weapon for training practice, but one used these wooden swords for the actual combat against a live blade or real *Nippon-to.* It is known that the *boken* were used in what is called *shinken shobu,* or a duel to the death with real swords. Empty-hand defense practiced against a sword as it was done in this *dojo* is known as *muto.*

The opposing wall to my left held six-foot staffs called *bo* or *kon.* These racks are called *yari-kake,* designed for spears or *kon.* These *kon* were an ancient type of weapon used as defensive tools against swords, halberds, and spears called *yari.*

I learned very quickly from observation that nothing either ordinary or out of the ordinary was done without proper etiquette. In Japanese this is called *reigi* or *reigisaho.* I paid strict notice to the severity of what was being taught and practiced in this *dojo.* Each student, lower grades or advanced, responded to the master's commands with immediate action at high speed, as if each task held utmost importance. Conformity based upon time-honored traditions was strong, as if these students resembled the predecessors of the ancient *samurai.* My mind spun with incarnations of the antiquated past played out in the present. I noticed details in the most minute fashion and came to understand that these fine points created an unbeatable mind as the martial artist or *Budoka* became one with the self or inner way and not an example of a careless fighter who is only set on winning. Winning is good only if it is backed with a clear, precise blend of technique and dominant spirit.

I did not know if I would be allowed to match myself with other students or attempt my expertise in any manner. What I was experiencing was ancient ritualized tradition in every sense. I became mesmerized by complete obsession as my spiritual side seemed to overtake my presence while being drawn still deeper into the world of this Oriental philosophy.

As I sat in the formal seated position, I noticed my legs beginning to fall asleep. First some discomfort, then no feeling at all. I could see these iron minds of will lined up like West Point cadets beginning to move from their unshakable positions. Directly in front of me, a student was motionless, then he began to rock ever so slowly to the right and left and forward or back. I watched sweat drip down his temple in a rush as the same happened to me. A moment later he fell over, passing out from the heat and pressure. I knew that losing face of any sort would cost him dearly in future training sessions at this *dojo*. Two junior instructors helped him to the *idiguchi* for fresh air. The head *sensei* spoke softly but firmly about ways to initiate specific practice routines.

To his right were stacks of roof tiles, the same ones I noticed earlier on the houses. He mentioned the power of *Budo* as something very special and possessed by us all. What was this secret essence that can be focused and generated to do tremendous amounts of damage as well as heal? Sensei quietly translated for me in a broken fashion, attempting not to create a disturbance. To the left of center as I sat were what appeared to be stacks of cut-up wood piled high. No doubt these would be broken in the standard use of *tameshiwari*. The information overload was beginning to take hold of me as I too began to falter in my seated position and in my thinking. To my relief, we were all asked to rise and stretch for five minutes before moving on. As I rose, I found I could not move my legs. Sensei noticed me attempting to get up and quickly came to my rescue before I made a fool of myself. Attempting to climb back to a standing position, I almost fell over on top of another student next to me. He stared back at me surprised. Sensei said that future practice will consist of seated position before class every day for at least fifteen minutes to condition my legs for this type of ordeal. A few moments later, my legs came back to life and I moved to increase their use as my blood circulation returned to normal.

All the students paired off, stretched, and moved throughout the *dojo* but not one word was spoken. Only the sound of feet against the *tatami* mats and the heavy breathing of those present was heard. Many of the spectators in the small *genkan* were somehow equally alert and orderly, gaining insight to their cultural right. Many older students or relatives of the headmaster sat in the cross-legged position, Burmese style, perceptively maintaining a calmness I never experienced in any group gathering. Each and every spectator focused their gaze upon the master *sensei* as though to honor his demanding excellence and benevolent guidance.

I never quite knew the name of this Japanese person. I believe it was Yamashita or Yamaguchi Sensei or something similar; he was a *Nihonjin* of enormous proportions. He looked as though he could have been previously employed as a *sumo* wrestler from Tokyo in the weight range of approximately 300 pounds or more. Over six feet tall, a scar across the left side of his face, shaven head, short neck, and piecing eyes, he was a warrior of admirable proportions who stood vigilance in this twentieth-century *dojo* in the suburbs of Yokusuka. Beyond any question, this was his *dojo*. My mind feared the consequences of facing this adversary in some alley if his soul went bad. Written on the left side of his *keikogi* were the *kanji* bearing the meaning of what I believe to be *Shotokan*. *Shotokan* means "the way of calligraphy training hall." Bold red characters emphasized the importance of protecting his colors in the traditional manner. Other *kanji* ran down his lapel expressing his position in the *Shotokan* system or other important details. As powerful as he may have seemed, his manner was one of peaceful grace with explosive power in reserve.

While watching what unfolded as a display of dominant *ki* (internal energy) based on years of exact skill, I knew I would conquer all the fears I harbored and fulfill my newfound destiny. Today in my history book, my Sensei and I were privileged guests to ageless *tameshiwari* we both would always remember.

A command was given for all of us to line back up and take positions on the *tatami*. This time we were allowed to sit in the cross-legged position, so we and the spectators were given the opportunity to remain in relative comfort. I was delighted by this option. Several advanced students gathered in the front of the *taijo* to prepare for the first exhibition of the afternoon. The heat and humidity seemed to suck all the oxygen out of the air. Yamashita Sensei walked close to us in response to an elder sitting nearby who signaled him with a private question. This gentlemen looked ancient and wise—perhaps another martial artist in a similar system or different martial art like *kenjitsu*. I noticed the *sensei's* hands appeared as if they could be used to drive nails through two-by-fours. The calluses on the side of his hand used as the knife-hand in striking were equally hardened for contact. I could only assume he spent hours outside in the back of the *dojo* performing techniques on the *makiwara* or better yet, dismembering a tree.

It was later in my own story that I would find out how significant this rudimentary training tool would become in every aspect of my practice. It would become the life and breath of my do and the very blood of my existence.

Later on in the day after the demonstrations, I had the opportunity to drift outside behind the *dojo* to examine the *makiwara* used by a few senior students. Anchored deep in the ground, the striking posts were lined up at different heights. I watched as one of the students launched kicks with the ball of his foot to one shorter than the others. Time-worn hemp circled each post, ragged from thousands of thundering strikes day in and day out. It all appeared to be their form of active meditation and served as means to connect with the real and unreal in life. I discovered the reality as found in *Budo* was one of finding the real self through discipline via this type of practice as well as other means to gain pure enlightenment or *satori*. It was difficult to maintain, but simple to surmise that one must never give it up.

It was up to the student to take the teachings and cultivate the skill in practice methods in order to shape his own destiny. One had to say, "Open the door slowly and pragmatically until skill awakened the soul." This awakening was perpetuated by the development of the non-stopping mind or no-mind as advocated by Takuan, the Zen priest-monk. This realization was of the nature that the sword and Zen are one, and it applies to *aikido, tai chi chuan,* or any other martial art. The only way the universe could be understood was by direct experience acquired through one's own training.

Many long planks filled the courtyard as a deck. Each was connected and beveled in a unique way so that they fit together with painstaking care and uniformity. Everything was an art and the end result of every task was in a sense very fascinating to behold. All was *kata*—the way of doing things. My understanding of *kata* was based on the forms practice in *karate,* but through an explanation in the Japanese culture, it must be understood that everything is *kata.* Every task no matter how simple was known to have a degree of *kata* within it. The details and particulars of each action were ultimately important and refined, depending on its relation to life, i.e., the culture.

Strange and exciting as it may seem, it was my hope to return and use the *makiwara* with my Sensei's permission and be allowed to perform my *waza* if the *dojo sensei* would allow me. I knew little of the temperament found in the gentle giant who ran this "ship." Somehow I must come to know him more. I still experienced great darkness and needed to gain clearer enlightenment.

I knew I needed to study under original sources of *Budo.* This intrinsic knowledge was truly what I had to gain and must never allow myself to be misled in the false mastery of things I could not truly understand. Falsehood brought on by an insecure ego was like a cancer to me. An experience of deceitful nonsense based on another's incorrect or asinine ideas was already filling our world with charlatans and illegitimate technicians. I wanted to become whole, real, and original. It was unfortunate for those who possessed great ability to get sucked into the pretense they were learning the genuine, direct transmission of legitimate *bujitsu* or *Budo.* If I ever took a wrong turn, I would have to find the path once again.

But for now, the exhibition continued. At this point, several roof tiles were stacked one upon the other until four stacks lined the front of the *taijo,* each with more tiles than the one next to it. Five, seven, ten, and then approximately twelve consecutively were ready for the break. Yamashita Sensei went through a period of deep breathing techniques for a brief moment which seemed to make everyone freeze in motion. Then lining up in front of the first stack, he gauged his distance, let out an ear-piercing *kiai,* and with a thunderous smash destroyed the entire pile of tiles with a reverse punch. Quickly shifting to the next stack, he once again cocked back his knife hand, this time holding it skyward above his head as if to cut like a sword. Then momentarily waiting for his *ki* to reaffirm, he sliced the air with an explosive charge backed by *kiai,* smashing the second mass of tiles. Rubble lay everywhere from the blast.

Looking down at my hands, I found one of my fists clenched tight, resting on the *tatami* with knuckles white as I squeezed. Moving it, I noticed a sweat mark where it had been sitting. My gaze covered the entire *dojo,* and I noticed everyone leaning slightly forward as if to catch some energy from the *sensei*'s action. The sweet smell of *tatami* filled the air. The aroma was more obvious than earlier, as though the spirit of *Budo* became even more present. Spectators seemed to stare in awe, but no applause or reference to his success was acknowledged. I knew then that silence was the reward, and the stillness filled with the master's emotional esprit permeated the essence of all.

Most everyone was awestruck. Yamashita Sensei then started to move toward the next break, where the most tiles were piled. As he slowly approached his task, he kept repeating a word which became familiar to me later on. *"Hissho nashi—Hissho nashi"*—decisive victory or no failure. Over and over he repeated these words as he prepared for his next *tameshiwara* of greatest magnitude. I believe at least twelve to fifteen tiles were braced against one another, supported by two large cement blocks to lift them higher off the ground. The top reached approximately waist level. It may sound strange, but I felt that he was in the process of fighting a battle of internal warfare. I could see his opponents as they circled around him. Indeed, it was a *samurai* engaged in the center of mortal war for one brief moment in time, a conflict of spiritual survival.

I intensified my gaze, tightened my stomach, and braced my muscles for the next break. Everything stood still; even time seemed to have stopped.

My eyes moved to the back door facing the *makiwara* courtyard, where several small sparrows and finches filled the branches of a tree hidden among the cherry blossoms. Silence was dominant except for the universal cadence of Yamashita Sensei's voice. Once again in poetic motion, he positioned himself differently, stretching sideways for what appeared to be an elbow break. There was no indecision. He was primed to amass all the positive *ki* possible for what stood before him in battle.

I envisioned conflict. *Seven samurai stood before him, swords (daisho), both daito and wakizashi in hand, each with razor-sharp steel bearing the soul of Bushido. Each samurai swore an oath and now armed their minds with an objective, an ultimatum to attack in an exact moment.* It felt as though he were ready to do battle in the midst of actual warfare. The air felt as though it would crack and break at the first instant of attack, when all those surrounding him would achieve their destiny in unison to attempt to destroy the opponent. We all waited.

A thundering *kiai* filled the *dojo,* as body and spirit in equal motion jumped into the air and then returned to meet the mountain of earth tiles. His elbow sliced through each tile as though they were made of dreams until the bottom piece fell to the *tatami.* Tile, debris, and dust flew everywhere, filling the surrounding area from his weaponless attack. All the *samurai* who challenged his life lay dead around him. My mind played tricks on me that instant, while my spirit built up momentum as this memory branded itself in my thoughts. Those observing let out a sigh of relief and awe while several students rushed to offer assistance in the clean-up and to prepare the next demonstration of precipitous power found in true *karate-do.*

I knew this was the challenge of the self, a decisive victory for the *Budoka* who seeks inner light from severe physical discipline through the forging of the spirit. This spiritual practice perfects technique and self as one. Though the human being has physical limitations, the universal mind and spirit can continue throughout one's life. So each dedicated *Budoka* of his or her art seeks to know the self as the action becomes the endeavor to be continued through one's existence. This reality is in itself final.

Over the entrance way to the *sensei*'s office, I noticed more *kanji*, later finding out it represented Funakoshi Sensei's words, "You must practice a lifetime to learn *karate;* there is no limit." This came from his principles, called *Shoto Niju Kun.*

Everything I perceived was esoteric. Each time I touched an object or felt a specific mood rush through my veins, I knew that the *dojo* was truly a sacred place of the mind and body. Outside, the birds that left the tree in terror now returned to echo their songs of life. Slowly, ever so slowly, petals from the cherry blossoms drifted to the deck below the tree, each in its own way, each with a specific pattern. Nature continued to unfold.

Next, as many as seven students began to assist in the subsequent demonstration. First, three senior students gathered planks of wood and stacked them. In all I counted six planks scheduled for destruction in the next performance. The first few students placed themselves so the planks of wood were held in hand by all three at approximately chest level from their bodies — arms extended and locked to form a rigid target. All three stood side by side to create a barrier. Then two more junior students were placed behind the first three and forced their weight against the ones in front to add stability in the break.

The *sensei* then began to step off the distance needed to execute a lunging side kick from about seven feet away. So here you have a wrecking machine of several hundred pounds who would launch himself as a human projectile bent on destroying anything in its way. All six planks would be turned to kindling in a matter of moments. To my surprise, Yamashita Sensei motioned for two other black belts to draw two razor-sharp *katana* (swords) from their protective *saya* (scabbards). They were instructed to hold them level as they stood next to the front outside men holding the boards. They were to place the blades lengthwise and even with the top and bottom of the front board. This would make the center of the target he would strike most accurate, and one inch off meant that a major part of him could be cleanly shaven off.

In clear terms, you have a target seven to eight feet away six inches thick, backed by pillars to hold them in place. Two sharp *Nippon-to* positioned strategically to slice anything that makes contact with their blade, and one forbidding and profound warrior ready for peril. I disciplined my mind for the next battle.

Next Yamashita Sensei started to shout loudly the words *"Issho, Issho, Issho"*—which I found out later means "one life." The reference meant you have but one life in order to accomplish your deeds to perfect the way or path, to draw the most from one's efforts in the most forceful way, or what may be termed *gendo-ryoku* or driving force. *Budoka* were taught that each moment in one's life is to be revered as the last, and one must strive to squeeze as much understanding into each. I looked deep within myself to find my personal worth. I needed more fulfillment, more individual recognition that my path, my way, was the best suited for me. Everything had to be earned in order to gain excellence. I knew that my experiences found in this *dojo* as in so many others would allow me to see the tip of the iceberg, not in an illusory sense, but in a way that would press me on to gain all the sincere peacefulness I hoped to find.

Yamashita Sensei cleared the air with his voice and appeared to look like a primitive cat, then with lightning speed sprang through the crackling atmosphere with a thundering *kiai.* In a blur, his foot slid between the swords missing by a fraction, then made contact with the front plank and drove through the rest as they exploded into the air in random directions. Blowing through brittle wood, the knife blade of his foot reached the first student senior holding the planks and caught his midsection. The rear two junior students were thrown like projectiles out the back door onto the deck on their rear ends. The penetration was so intense that the one senior who took a hit as the *sensei's* foot passed through the boards sat on the *tatami* holding his chest. Moments more spectacular than those before passed while this giant of a man settled down to respectfully bow to his students and then the entire class, which was captivated by the excitement.

Several more demonstrations took place that day, performed by his students and seniors all set on achieving triumphant tasks which involved the spirit and inner power, *ki,* of karate-do. It was afterward when most students left the *dojo* that sensational day that I was allowed to walk the grounds and training area to experience my emotional passion of things *Budo.* Sensei was invited into Yamashita's *jimusho* (office) to partake in *sake* and relate stories of *karate-do.* I took great advantage of this privileged time to inspect many of the *Shotokan's* art and to gain various practice ideas.

Walking past the weapons wall, I heard a *thud, thud, thud* coming from the patio where everyone performed *makiwara* practice. Stepping around the corner into the *idiguchi,* I observed an advanced black belt using a bottle in the most strange way. He had taken a large Sapporo beer bottle, filled it with sand, and while holding the neck of the bottle, slammed it repeatedly into his shins. Up and down he hammered, from one side to the other in long durations before shifting to the other shin and back again. His shins must have been like concrete, and it was only a short time later that I found out just how hard they were.

I had just finished drinking a small bottle of *sake* with the *senseis* (in which I was greatly honored) when we heard a roaring *kiai.* Mixed with the *kiai* was a loud crack, followed by the hum of approval from a few students who remained in the *dojo.* Sensei Yamashita said in broken English, "It's only my senior student punishing Mickey Mantle today. You know how the *Nihonjin* love baseball." I did not quite understand his meaning and asked if I could see. He waved me to go out in the *taijo* and watch. As if I had not seen enough today already, to my surprise the student who was using the beer bottle outside the *dojo* earlier was now breaking baseball bats with his shin. Two students would hold the bats at separate ends, then on personal command, the *karateka* would launch a roundhouse kick or front kick, smashing the previously useful bat into two pieces.

I thought to myself, what method would be used to block and defend against such a formidable weapon? Smiles on the student's faces appeared for the first time that day in gratification of their *tameshiwari* success. I could hardly believe what I was witnessing. The bats themselves were more like hand-turned clubs, but still very hard.

Soon afterward, Sensei and I bid all the remaining students and Yamashita Sensei farewell. Exchanging respectful bows, we left the *dojo* and slipped our shoes back on outside. "Sensei Yamashita requests us to return on our next visit in port to practice and try *kumite* free-sparring," said Sensei.

Sensei Love looked for a sign of excitement, but I seemed perplexed by everything I just witnessed and said, "Do I have a chance to win, do you think?"

Sensei looked down the long narrow street we had begun to walk and said, "Jack, if you encounter a mountain in the path of your journey, do you stop and go home?"

I said, "No, Sensei."

"When you climb each mountain, you will be stronger yet and foster the indomitable spirit! Now let's go back to Yokusuka for beer, lunch, and *sake*. We have much to discuss, and by the way, Yamashita Sensei asked me to return before we leave port next week for a special session on throws. It's called the 'Ten Thousand Throws' practice and you're invited." My jaw dropped.

Chugi—Loyalty

CHAPTER FOUR

Ring of Strategy

The CVA-63 aircraft carrier steamed its way toward Hong Kong harbor for R & R. Shore leave would be a welcome break for everyone who had maintained some level of sanity at sea over the last forty-five days. The seas became calm and everything possible was expedited to clean the ship during this downtime as flight operations came to a standstill. As one learns, everything must be perfect in order to pass inspection, and our preparations for shore duty were no exception.

I sat quietly on the steel nonskid deck positioned on one of the elevators that carry fighter aircraft up to the flight deck, from which they depart to unleash their terrible force on the unfortunate. Over the noonday sea, flying fish raced across the water in search of food as the carrier cut the ocean surf. Gentle dolphins swam, jumped, and kept pace with our movement. At a distance I could see the "tin can" (destroyer escort) pacing us on our way to Hong Kong. Laden with antiaircraft missiles and equipped with submarine countermeasures, ominous as a predator, the tin can was famous for its high-tech performance and top speed and infamous for its lack of amenities. I often wondered how those aboard kept from going crazy with so little to do. I reminded myself that at least I had all the amenities of my ship. As vast as my ship was, I was still driven stir crazy at times. So there I sat with my starched jeans and denim shirt, flaunting my master-at-arms badge, wondering what the night had in store for me. Perhaps one of the nightly movies or a comfortable evening writing home. A day rarely went by that I would miss placing ink to paper and expressing my need to see the faces of those back home.

All the ship's personnel were in a cleaning frenzy because of the big event unfolding in two days. It seemed the U.S.O. was presenting a show on our ship in conjunction with the Da Nang Air Base. Arrangements were underway. This show was one of the biggest: Bob Hope would be there with his entourage, and among the guests was Ms. Joey Heatherton. The Navy boys and Marines would be going out of their minds for a few hours during the night to come. We all were excited about the event.

Just then Sensei Love came up from behind and said, "Jack, I've got some good news for you. The night before the show, the ship is presenting a smoker and as intermission I will be putting on an exhibition, so it looks like you and a couple of the other advanced students will support me as sparring partners. So get together with me later to discuss the event."

"O.K. Sensei," I replied.

A smoker is a term used to denote a competitive fighting match held in an area or boxing ring that pits so-called street fighters or would-be boxers against one another. Everyone wore gloves and specific rules controlled some of the action. From time to time, the rule was that there were no rules. Several fighters from the boxing club would be matched up against their opponents in an all-out, one-to-one battle. Many competitors were considered good from previous battles or amateur contests, but most had little training and fell to exhaustion quickly in the first round.

The ones who survived were usually powerful and found the advantage of a lucky punch. In the United States, these events are described as "Tough Man Contests" and sometimes offer cash awards. Usually the award gained on board the ship was a sense of victory and a means for everyone to gamble, which promoted the event in a more electrifying fashion for 2,500 crazy sailors and Marines.

I sat back down on the steel deck, turning my gaze to the afternoon sun dancing on the sea. I collected my vanishing thoughts and focused on the upcoming battle demonstration, uncertain at the punishment I would be submitted to at the hands of my *sensei*. Martial arts had become a way of life and a means to attack my fears and strengthen my spirit. I would do as I was told, practice with the will of a thousand warriors, and conquer that which came between me and my art. The practice had become the way. I never questioned my teacher. I just did what I was told, and the enlightenment appeared at brief moments while I was under the hammer.

In all aspects, I learned simply and clearly to get it and get it right. That was real, that was battle. Unassuming, I trained hard to become the best. Sensei had departed with the closing words, "Better sharpen your hook punch."

Focusing on my next task, my stomach told me that food would be the first move toward practice. It would be a half-dozen eggs and a good juicy steak for the protein I needed later in the day. Good food was never lacking in the Navy. Crossing the hangar bay, I saw many squids sitting and playing cards in the ready rooms strung along the inside of the bay. A bodybuilder friend of mine, Washington, stopped to talk to me about the upcoming event. Of course I was surprised to hear him mention that Sensei was going to put some pain into the chain of events that night, and I laughed, saying, "We all have to die sometime."

Minutes passed, then I made my way to the mess hall down below. I couldn't understand what Sensei meant by practicing the hook. Was he setting a specific stage I needed to be aware of, or making me conscious of a weak link in my combative proficiency? Eating quickly, I decided I would go back to the *dojo* and start practicing my hook. But first, digestion had to take a firm hold if my food was to stay in place.

"That's it. I will grind the afternoon away focused on one blow, the roundhouse hooking punch," I told myself. Arriving an hour or so later, I changed into my *keikogi* for an intense punching workout that might shift the wave of the battle I would soon enter. I was unsure where this would lead but knew that it couldn't damage the outcome. If anything, I knew that my tempering would prove itself worthy for the upcoming night or later in the future.

"The mind is the greatest tool in battle, but the body—that which is slave to the mind—must be prepared in every regard. A warrior should not go to sleep before reflecting on what he should have done that he might have neglected and on what he has to do the next day. Looking back, one needs to know he tempered the weak links in the chain, as only in battle will the true test rely on the past events and that which transpires."

It is easy to forget about danger when secure or chaos in times of order. Even during times of peace, one must not abandon the military mindset. An old Latin phrase reminds us "He who desires peace prepares for war." Those who disregard this knowledge are doomed in time of combat, be it large-scale or man-to-man. One must learn to be aware of the unexpected, to expect anything, and to put the self in a place other than the norm, looking at the ways of how not to be defeated.

In this way, one can be ready for the defensive counter needed to repel a charge. Attacking only can lead to a blind attack, so it is important that an attack be launched with victory in mind based on use of defensive tactics.

I first wrapped my hand tightly, then taped it solid, should it give under the intense pressure. My knuckles were stronger now, but I was sometimes overzealous in repetition. I lived to be extreme.

In the training area, a five-inch steel pipe ran from deck to deck placed very close to the wall, perhaps an inch or so. The striking pad that was glued to the wall next to it was made of compressed life preserver packing material placed layer on top of layer, then sewn together by one of Sensei's students from the tailor's shop. Life preserver for contact and survival. I thought that was rough poetry.

It was solid, rough, and glued to the steel wall. Shaped in a square approximately twelve by twelve and four to six inches thick, the pad had a deep circular pit formed in the center similar to an old-style catcher's mitt. This allowed the largest of knuckles to penetrate deeply as one buried his fist in the target while the others were forced tightly together in support. A great training device to use anywhere if one could affix it properly. The steel pipe, on the other hand, forced one to cover the face and take precautions against wild, sloppy maneuvers while punching, lest your face crash into the pipe. In effect, the cover hand naturally learned to protect the face while advancing with the punches. A target was placed on both sides of the pipe so one could develop either punch to the maximum. One could also grab the pipe as if grabbing the opponent's chest or shoulder in what would seem to work as a counter-move. Excellent training device!

I sat in a formal position and began to meditate. Strange as it was, silence now fell everywhere, with no flight noise above or major evidence of war activity taking place around me. Dead silence fell everywhere. Others were off relaxing with subservient tasks, but I was preparing to submit myself to personal war. Correct preparation meant the battle was half fought.

Then I rose and took my position. Sliding in, I began to hook punch gradually, then applying full power in an attempt to clear my mind and find my correct *ki*. Sweeping my fist out wide and circling inward, my hammer found its mark. Several hundred blows rang out against the steel, and I was sure the thundering could be heard some distance away. Punching, breathing, and contracting my entire body, I powered onward to find the ultimate power hook disrupting the pervasive silence. Never stopping for a moment, there I was, at pure harmony and in accord with myself. Later I found out from my present-day Sensei that this is called *sabi shiori*. This is the relentless vigilance and sound of your feet moving against the mats, or the deep rhythmic breathing of your lungs as powerful air is sucked inward, then forcibly expelled out, and the echo of the wall as it goes on and on. You became powerful and could not be stopped. Only the driving force, or *gendo-ryoku*, kept you going. In the traditional *Budo*, this perseverance was called *ryomi*.

"*Ryomi* translates simply as 'reflection.' One must learn through his training to never allow enthusiasm to escape one's mind. Perfection of technique must be a tireless effort and a means for flawlessness of mind and body through movement. One of the most important aspects of a *shihan*—or one who models for the rest—is to never give up, not to accept failure. To keep in mind the words, 'I don't think it's quite good enough yet,' and continue to repeat *Renma*." (*Renma* translates as "to polish one's skill.")

A brilliant master works intently on the most simple aspects of his practice. He must create an incessant willingness to critically observe his progress, reflect upon it, and strive to be better no matter how long he practices or how perfect his technique may appear. This is *ryomi,* a continuous process of self-evaluation for the martial artist or *Budoka,* or anyone who desires to make anything worthwhile of their existence.

Determination is the means to master the *waza* (technique). Be it a sweep, a *judo* throw *(nage),* or a cut of the blade with the *Nippon-to,* the Japanese sword—the essence is in the complete movement.

Fists swinging against steel, mind for body, breath for life, I drove myself toward the limits of my endurance. Onward I hooked, switching from side to side, from pad to pad, crimson beginning to seep from my wrappings. Onward I rushed, pragmatically, until I dropped to the floor in exhaustion. Focus, I told myself—victory was at my door and now I must find total clarity. I kneeled and dropped my head to the mat, feeling my guts wrench, fighting my desire to be gallant and noble. My disposition was stronger and my passion reeled in dynamic accord. I shouted in one breath, "Watch out world, here I come!" Just then Sensei walked into the *dojo.* In a shot I was on my feet at attention and bowed, "Hello, Sensei."

He replied, "Jack, relax and go rest. Tomorrow we'll work things out for the captains and his soldiers."

I answered, "O.K. Sensei, I understand." Sensei meant that we would prepare a demonstration and exhibition for the ship's personnel and one to please the best captain. I was sure the whole program would include combative engagement only. No flash or fancy displays; just traditional full contact.

To the showers I headed. Tomorrow would be a new day. In the days to come our ship moved closer to the port of Hong Kong. All the ship's personnel seemed to relax more in anticipation of the show and the smoker. I spent more time with Sensei than ever before practicing light *kumite* and felt things falling neatly into place as a sense of confidence grew. Training sessions lasted long into the night hours and were more informal, which allowed lengthy evaluations. In the process we all seemed to gain a more esoteric understanding of what we had committed ourselves to. Bruises, lumps, and cuts all became part of the program as the smell of Tiger Balm filled the air after workouts.

Angelo and Scot, my *dojo* buddies, were constantly paired off with me. Wave after wave of battle forced us to evaluate each other's tactics and occasional frustrations, but a fighting team we had become. We prepared for ultimate brutal warfare, became obsessed with victory.

> *Bun Bu Ryodo*—The arts of war and peace. The arts of war and peace are like two wheels of the cart which, lacking one, will have difficulty in standing. Naturally, the arts of peace are used during times of tranquility and those of war during times of confusion, but it is most essential to not forget the military during peaceful times nor to disregard scholastics during time of war. When the master of a province feels that the world is in peace and forgets the arts of war, first military tactics will fall into disuse, the warriors of his clan will naturally become effeminate and lose interest in martial ways, the martial arts will be neglected, the variety of weapons will be insufficient, weapons handed down through the generations will become rusty and rot, and there will be nothing of any use during times of emergency. If the Way of the Warrior is thus neglected, ordinary military tactics will not be established. If a military situation were to suddenly arise there would be panic and confusion, consultation would be unprepared for, and the establishment of strategy would be difficult. When one has been born into the house of a military commander, he should not forget the Art of War even for a moment.
> —Kuroda Nagamasa (1568–1623), *samurai* general

This trip would be our last one overseas, since we were all scheduled for separation from the service in the next eight to nine months. Four years of dreadful war games would soon come to an end for me and for the country. Undoubtedly, the martial arts fire would continue to blaze strongly. Lying in my rack I stared at the ceiling. There was no shortage of time while at sea, and I had inscribed the words "To ceaselessly go beyond" on the ceiling, staring me in the face. After much tossing and turning thinking of what to expect over the next couple of days, I fell into a deep sleep.

When I awoke, it was five in the morning and the ship was quiet, cutting through the South China Sea, heading for the port of Hong Kong. There was a refueling and supplies tanker which we would take stores from while en route, and then head straight for mainland China and Hong Kong. Sensei woke me and the other boys. We were surprised at the early morning roust, but as we learned over time, anything was possible during the practice of *Budo*. We all met in the game room and filed one after another through the passageway maze to the mess hall.

I was quiet, as were the others, knowing some arduous task was before us. Everyone was still burnt from the prior days of battle, the continuous hardline practice, and little rest.

Finishing breakfast, Sensei said, "Meet me on the fantail with your uniforms in one hour. I want to work out details for the fight demonstration with all of you." Replying, we departed and met later on that hour. The fantail was usually a messy place where all the ship's litter and garbage is thrown overside. Now spotless for inspection (the Marines must have used the place for cleaning competition), everything was steel gray, shining, and ready for us to use. Quickly slipping into our training uniforms *(gi)*, we began stretching in the warm humid morning sea mist.

The powerful engines of the aircraft carrier churned the water into uncontrolled foam that left an enormous wake in the calm sea. The water looked dark and flat as though you could walk on it, creating an eerie feeling as the sunless sky began to grow lighter with the new dawn approaching.

With enough light to see our way, Sensei instructed us to form a wide circle and in a slow-motion cadence attack with an even pace at one's discretion in the appropriate controlled manner. Sensei Love remained in the center. All began with the ritual bow and then moved like cats, stalking from one side to the other. Sensei instructed us to relax and move with simple fluid motions, never changing the pace. This type of movement allows one to observe one's presence and focus on the details such as fighting combinations and smooth rhythm, creating a useful process of execution. Wearing only our *keikogi* bottoms and *obi,* there we were, meeting the rising sun as it broke the horizon on the sea, barechested young warriors doing what most people thought was crazy.

Sensei moved in and out of our attacks, like a panther in the dense forest, seldom touching us as we launched our slow-motion dance of punches and kicks. This was the multiple preparation of what was to come later at the smoker. Practice lasted approximately an hour and finished as the entire morning sky lit up with the intense tropical heat.

We all knew the demonstration wouldn't be in slow motion, nor would we. It would be hard and fast while a thousand guys watched and expressed their response in the hangar bay during a day which would become history. The pressure would unquestionably be severe, and because of the frenzy found during multiple attacks, the possibility of uncontrolled contact was justifiable. We would be striking full power.

Later in the afternoon, the smoker arena was constructed. The aircraft that remained on the ship were maneuvered to other areas, where their silver skin and colors were polished to a bright luster. The decks around the ring were bristling clean of aviation gas and oil. Here the ship's crew would sit and watch. The ring was covered in canvas as traditional boxing rings were, and the stars and stripes were draped around the turnbuckles and ropes, displaying the American colors. Powerful lights dangled and stretched from the hangar bay ceiling over the ring, as did a microphone used by the master of ceremonies to present the events. Everything was close to completion, and I moved quickly to my compartment where I would rest and prepare for the event. Few people were there, and it seemed everyone found a place to escape for privacy. I did the same and meditated for a length of time.

Some of the boxing events were scheduled to begin at sundown, and the martial arts portion would take place at intermission. Amazing how things esoteric are looked upon as entertainment for most people. I thought of the ordeals and triumphs found in the relentless practice and inexhaustible dedication to *Budo*. I frowned at the thought that those watching our display of skill had little if any idea of the true substance created in our dedication. There are those who act and those who live in the illusion of becoming. How typical that so few really get it and strive to ultimate levels of universal *satori*. I queried how many allowed petty values or superficial goals to suck them dry of the intangible gifts found through this life-giving means, a channel to the ultimate beauty of peace based on a violent science. Two sides of the same coin.

We all met at six o'clock in a ready room off to the side of the hangar bay and the event. I peered out of the door to see a wild crowd of spectators screaming and clapping their hands as two pugilists fought brutally on the canvas. Boxing gloves smashed faces and midsections as the two gladiators clashed in grips with one another. The lights shining on the ring made it look as though we were far away from the Viet Nam War and helped to block out our memories. Only the excitement remained. It was hypnotizing. I felt the blood start pumping through my veins, and my mind felt reluctant about the series of events soon about to unfold.

The fights wore on as time grew short. Then Sensei stepped through the doorway.

"Gentlemen, change up, it's about time."

"*Hai*, Sensei," we all responded at the same moment. Acting like *samurai* from the Tokugawa era, we began the ceremonial process of changing into our war gear and primed our *seishin* for extreme battle. We would be under the most decisive pressure to perform well by challenging our very own teacher's exact warrior mentality and skill. Even more so, Sensei had a reputation to stand behind his means, which meant we wouldn't be allowed to overshadow or obstruct his tactical prowess. Things were about to heat up. I glanced out of the doorway once again, only to see some Marine being carried away in a stretcher. No doubt he wished he were somewhere else. I thought, *Oh boy!*

I found a fairly quiet place. The only sounds were those which drifted in from the hangar bay. The crowd was in an uproar and the pace of individual duels was growing quickly, as if two armies clashed in a war. In a kneeling position, I began to clear my young warrior mind and find a universal moment of peace and clarity. Just an instant to search for my inner strength and the simplicity of overcoming my newfound fears of that which was about to come.

> The Zen mind is the military mind. It is comparatively simple and not at all addicted to philosophizing. The discipline of Zen is simple, direct, self-reliant, self-denying; its ascetic spirit goes well with the fighting spirit. The fighter is to be always single-minded with one object in mind: To go straight forward in order to crush the enemy is all that is necessary for him. He is therefore not to be encumbered in any possible way, be it physical, emotional, or intellectual.
>
> —D. T. Suzuki

"The worst enemy of our life is cowardice, and how can I escape it?" the young Hojo regent, Tokimune, asked the Chinese Zen master Bukko.

"Cut off the source whence cowardice comes," Bukko responded.

"Where does it come from?"

"It comes from Tokimune himself," said Bukko.

"Above all things, cowardice is what I hate most," said Tokimune. "How can it come out of myself?"

"See how you feel when you throw overboard your cherished self known as Tokimune," said Bukko. "I will see you again when you have done that."

"How can this be done?" asked Tokimune.

"Sit cross-legged in meditation and see into the source of all your thoughts which you imagine as belonging to Tokimune."

"I have so much of worldly affairs to look after and it is difficult to find spare moments for meditation," said Tokimune.

"Whatever worldly affairs you are engaged in, take them up as occasions for your inner reflection," Bukko responded, "and some day you will find out who this beloved Tokimune of yours is."

When the Mongol ships were sighted off the coast of Japan, Tokimune, dressed in full battle armor, hurried in to see his *sensei*.

"The great thing has come," he said.

"Can you avoid it?" Bukko asked calmly.

Tokimune stamped his feet and gave a tremendous *"Katsu!"* the great Zen shout which destroyed ignorance.

"A real lion cub, a real lion roar, " said Bukko, granting his approval. "Dash straight forward and don't look 'round."

Shooting upward, I rose from my kneeling meditation, *zazen,* with a powerful *kiai*. Everyone in the ready room snapped around to look at me, thinking I lost my mind. Those outside my view turned sharply, eyes wide open with startled surprise. Then I looked at Angelo and Scot standing dumbfounded. I said, "I'm ready. Let's go."

We lined up with Sensei in front of us as tradition requires, waiting for the ringmaster to announce the demonstration. Moments passed, the crowd thundered again, then a stream of eye-piercing floodlights turned on the ready room door and we all moved out down the break in the crowd toward the ring. No longer concerned about my course of action, I moved forward magically to execute my duty.

Fast-paced, we strutted proudly wearing our white *keikogi* and our emblems on the breast and back. Our colors were painstakingly sewn on the back so the crowd would remember the club name. Everyone was receptive and cheered us onward as we approached the ring. I felt as though I were a gladiator who at the instant of truth would sound off by saying, "We who are about to die salute you." This was a time I had never experienced before, as Sensei used monumental control during *kumite*. It felt as though I would become the only nail driven through the oak plank as fear moved throughout my entire body.

Envisioning the unfolding events and doubtful future, I continued toward the ring steadfast. It was my only choice. I must perform.

Angelo reached to open the ring ropes for Sensei, then Scot, and finally me. We all slipped through the ropes and into position. A great many knew Sensei because he had been on the *Kittyhawk* for several tours of duty. The crowd gave us a thundering welcome as the ring announcer introduced our demonstration. Then Sensei took the microphone, waited until those watching calmed down, and explained *kata* and *kumite* in short, specific detail, careful not to bore them, since they were there for action and few particulars.

Angelo and I would perform separate *kata,* then Sensei himself would do the same. I had been working on a specific *kata* for months preceding this surprise event, so my ability to withstand the pressure was somewhat improved.

> Practicing *kata* took long undistracted repetition which allowed the *sha* [practitioner] to cultivate one's powers of mental strength with the imaginary vision of fighting various *aite* [opponents]. This practice began and ended with a mind set of complete obsession within the realistic confines of battle. One must look at *kata* as the original lineage of our venerated mentors who came before us and a means to maintain original and pure representation of an entity historically conceived long before us. I could have one person watching or an entire army of thousands and still my *kata* would be uninterrupted during the execution of its nature. You needed no opponents, a *dojo,* a gym, or special circumstances to train in the way of *kata.* Its universal uniqueness allowed you to cultivate the clear enhancement of mind, body, and spirit in any atmosphere or under any conditions. It was in itself the actual means of self-development minus actual battle.

It would only be moments after our *kata* performance that each of us would take position and begin our multiple battle. My eyes turned to the sea, but nothing was visible out the hangar bay door, only the vast unending darkness that loomed during the quiet, lightless night. It was difficult to believe I stood in a world as one, learning to overcome my fears and be accountable for every action and every thought that entered and left my constantly changing mind. Eyes from every direction fixed themselves on our distinct moves, waiting to witness the failure of our concentration. There was none to be found. First Angelo moved through one of the basic Chinese *kempo*-fashion *kata*. I went next. If a mistake was found, I didn't want to see it. I was off in the stillness of my brain, a deep hidden corner which permitted no one to enter or any random thought to occur.

Sensei's *kata* was a monumental success. Blazing the canvas of the ring, he moved with the grace of a magician and the heart of a timeless *samurai*. Flawless in motion, he mesmerized the crowd with each exploding punch, kick, and exact action needed to complete his private battle. Finally in a masterful clarity, he ended with a thundering *kiai*. We all sat motionless waiting for the next event and Sensei's command.

Sensei motioned for us to take our positions around him. We began. Circling from side to side, we moved like warriors attempting to find the weak point of our enemy's defense. Cautious and wary in our manner, we spent more time waiting than committing ourselves to the first attack. No one wanted the indomitable wrath of any hammer to strike the anvil. It was Scot who launched the first attack by using a barrage of punches, but it was too late. No sooner had he begun his advance across the ring of fire than he took a fall from a spinning heel kick to the throat that sent him tumbling out under the ropes and onto the steel deck. A couple of sailors involuntarily helped to break his fall.

A moment later, Sensei launched a lightning blitz toward my corner as I bounced off the ropes in an adjacent direction. Angelo, now my partner, attempted to cover my defense by attacking Sensei's back. Driving a side kick with his long legs and the thrust of his six-foot-three-inch body, Angelo sent his kick thundering in. I thought Sensei missed noticing the attack, but it was clear he was ultimately ready. As he side-moved, he struck Angelo's calf with a sword hand strike, kicked his support leg behind him, and down Angelo went with a thud. I saw Angelo scramble for balance and safety with his guard from a ground position.

I followed pursuit with a series of roundhouse kicks and punches, all of which were blocked and simply forced away in every direction conceivable. Sensei was there, here, everywhere, and nowhere at once. I felt a bump on my head and a stinging on a rib, no doubt from flying punches used in countering my last assault. Disillusioned and now amazed at my ineptness of battle, I felt the strategy was to totally confuse us, frustrate our thinking, and teach us a lesson we'd never forget. Both Angelo and I were back on our feet circling and becoming winded in the extreme. The crowd was silent and astonished at the speed with which Sensei moved, and beyond any doubt, so was I.

We bounced off the ropes from side to side, turnbuckle to turnbuckle, then launched another thundering attack. This time Sensei decided to place us in total chaos. Now his powerful and lethal attack was to come. Sensei looked possessed and stopped in place. A second earlier he was in unbelievable nonstop action, but now he stood motionless and began to focus an unstoppable presence of *ki*. I knew something was coming, something he planned but kept a secret until the next moment.

I learned over time that though the inner secrets were revealed to the highest and most dedicated student, there was always something held in reserve. This was something the master finds for himself. This type of knowledge was found through the timeless study of tactics, and a tactician knows the value of experience and time. "Hold back the prize," I remembered hearing once.

If I made a fool of myself, so what, I could handle it. I was the student. But if Sensei finds out that I gave something away or allowed some stupid mistake to cost me my battle strategy, the consequences would be met with Sensei in the training hall at a time yet to come. That I didn't want.

In a flash, I envisioned failure. That was poison and could lead to *harakiri* or *seppuku*. Of course, no one was expected to cut open their abdomen these days for losing their honor, but the aftermath of mistakes in the presence of my teacher meant something similar. I had to give my whole mind to courage, and achieve my honor with class and swiftness, but how could it happen? In the *samurai* tradition, if my sword snapped, I could use my arms; if my arm broke or was cut, I could use my legs; and if my legs were dismembered, I could bite off a thousand enemies' ears. I could find a way to honor. I must conquer myself and turn the favor to sheer willpower. The soul and body were hardened like steel as a *samurai,* but victory must be won from within. Then a thousand enemies will fall at will.

I had to attack and make the first move, which could be fatal if I made the exact mistake Sensei was expecting. I spun out from rope to rope and, bouncing off a turnbuckle, charged full speed with everything I had to offer. Sensei was still; then, in the middle of my blitz, Angelo foolishly charged from his rear. In an instant Sensei disappeared and my side kick sizzled through the air and met Angelo in the solar plexus. He was out and I was dumbfounded. Angelo rolled to the edge of the ropes attempting to catch his wind. The crowd was on its feet roaring now and serious at the same time, witnessing Sensei's clever move.

I turned to see Sensei standing at attention in the middle of the ring. I looked into his eyes, I understood his masterful tactics, and recognized what I had known in the beginning: Sensei's will to win was far too great to overcome. I bowed and fell to my knees in exhaustion. Rising slowly, I humbly acknowledged his expertise and his control to overcome all odds. As we fought, my uniform top had been ripped off, and to my surprise I noticed heel marks and fist imprints in my flesh received during the numerous encounters. Strangely enough, any one of them could have broken a rib or ruptured a kidney, but it didn't. My knees were still intact as was my face, except for a cheek bruise and that goose egg on my head.

In awe of Sensei's *seishin,* we departed the ring with a standing ovation from well over a thousand servicemen. I was proud and honored to be part of such a noble group of individuals who helped me to finally witness the sliver of light at the end of the journey.

Neiyo—Honor

CHAPTER FIVE

Makiwara: The Straw Sheath Conflict

I remained in the *dojo* one night during the cold of winter for intense practice. This is referred to as *Shugyo Renshu,* or Enlightenment Training, which leads to purification *(misogi).* I could hear the wind blowing at the back door through the alleyway and awoke early in a chill. The night before was a battlefield of maximum training for the entire *dojo,* and I had continued late into the midnight hour with intense heavy-bag practice.

Trying to sleep, rolling over on my makeshift Japanese bed, I looked at the locker room back door. Humidity had built up in the *dojo* and I could see that frost and ice had formed on the steel alley door. A small patch of snow had even formed on the tile floor as witness to the wind chill and dropping temperatures outside. I shivered under the covers from the short four-hour snooze and wanted to return to the warmth of my dreams, but this training was an intense test of personal will and spirit.

My hands felt like mallets from the night's conditioning and hardening practice, which left them like stone. My special all-night practice was not yet over. I still had one final phase—*makiwara.* I rolled out of bed fighting my emotional resistance, cold, aches, and sleepiness. I worked my way over to the *makiwara* area in the practice hall. There shivering once again, I sat in *seiza,* lit some incense and a single candle, and meditated for a length of time. At first the morning cold drove deeply through my bones, then after a couple of moments I obtained a mental frame clear of any thought or vision. Distraction was nowhere to be found.

I breathed in deep abdominal breaths, then switched to hard aggressive exhaling. My mind was in the constant process of shaping itself for whatever my dreams demanded of me. Emotion played one role and common sense played another. The mind game was endless and continually questioning my determination to excel. Finishing some reflection upon my personal battles in life and what my present intention was to be, I rose and headed for the shower room. Flipping the light switch and the space heater on, I knew a good hot shower would make me feel better. How many other crazy martial artists did what I just did all night long? It was I who found the heart and the passion to stand for the punishment my teacher pushed me relentlessly to endure with practice after practice. I chose this way.

Night practice wasn't anything new, as I had witnessed many *karateka* overseas in Nippon fall out of bed because of the intense humidity in the midnight hour, then turn to training as a means to tolerate the heat. This was commonplace all over the tropics, whether it be the Philippines or Viet Nam. You just wanted to sleep. Difficulty came with a cockroach or spider crawling across your sweat-drenched chest or leg. A dog barking a click down the road was enough to test your nerves. Practice soothed the soul, as all martial artists preach and know. Night training allowed me to see things I couldn't always see during the day.

The thought of night practice in the humid tropics contrasted sharply with reality on this day. The Midwestern morning was harsh and uninviting, as it was so cold and unfriendly. Growing up in a cold climate isn't something one ever gets used to. My *karate* bones throbbed and I moved ever so slowly with my hands and legs slightly swollen from all the punching abuse I endured during my *shugyo* practice.

I pushed the front door open to experience nature for a moment. Five o'clock in the morning proved to be still and dark outside. The snow crunched under my feet with each step. Even though the winds were still now, my nose froze from the brisk cold air flowing through it. The workforce for the local auto industry had barely begun to move down the snow-packed pavement toward the assembly plants. Several GM or Buick automobile plants were within fifteen minutes, so most of my students were employees who had chosen *karate-do* as a means of self-discovery. I had good boys, all from hard-hitting football schools and homes that required discipline in the family.

The Viet Nam War was now far off, but it was coming to a close shortly after the *dojo* had opened, so many of my practitioners were vets home for the final time. Many of these guys loved the science of fighting and even more were hungry for the discipline now lacking since military separation. Warfare became their mainstay.

Bringing your life back together is a difficult task after being tuned to specific habits that are very much contrary to civilian society. My return was frustrating, like so many others who had come home expecting support and a hero's welcome. I had spent four long years in this war, for many unknown reasons, all of which were too confusing to make any sense of now. I had *karate-do,* that was one thing I knew for sure. It never lied to me, cheated, or stole from my heart. I could depend on the defined role it played in my life.

Quickly changing into my *keikogi,* I entered the practice hall once again. I would end my *shugyo* with *makiwara.* The salt brine solution I prepared was rich with crushed salt and a traditional Chinese herb. Now in *seiza,* the formal kneeling position used in my meditation, I washed my hands with the ancient blend. This was done for five minutes or so, then left to dry while I meditated once more. I deliberately filled my mind with concrete thoughts designed to foster adversity in preparation for my one-man war. One-man war on the *makiwara* was known in the *dojo* as *kojin-senso.* This battle against the opposing negative forces of the mind allowed one to blend with the powers of nature. You became a one-man army destined to conquer the walls of conflict as you struck the *makiwara* each time. In the early stillness of the half-lit training area, the *keikoba,* I would now face the ultimate partner and enemy in one continuous battle.

Holding *zazen,* or seated meditation, one can discover a clear and precise method for one's madness, then deliberately and pragmatically make oneself right. The entire process was designed to do what you might say, clear the debris, from the soul. Moments passed before I once again awoke from my *zazen*.

Looking down at my hands, I noticed the crystals of salt which had hardened, as though I had dipped my hands into a vat of flour. I rose to face the oak boards covered with old crimson blood. I would use the weapons of punching, striking, and kicking skills in a manner of ways to harden the battle blades of my martial art. One hour would pass before I stopped for any rest, and my pace would be that of an advancing war wagon. This would be the trial of the heart and the connection to the innerself. I poured some Chinese herbs similar to *dit dat dow* used for muscle bruises and inflammation over the wrist and forearms. Those areas would dry from the air as I hammered my way to victory. The *dojo* temperature must have been in the low fifties while I stretched before my conflict began. I longed for this solitary existence where I drove deep into the marrow of fortitude. My desire for anything was now replaced by enlightenment as I stood testimony to the *Bushido* code: Kill selfish desires, bravely face all enemies, keep a stainless mind and a sterling spirit in the face of all odds — this is *Bushido*.

I stepped closer to my challenge, silently waiting for engagement. Towering five feet strong stood the immortal *makiwara*. Two planks of clear polished oak rose before me in powerful coexistence, remaining still like a vigilant *samurai* guard meditating before a predetermined conflict. Both boards were rammed into a unique base of steel imbedded by six-inch steel reinforced bolts driven deep into concrete. The facing plank was wrapped with an old white *obi*, then reinforced with old-style hemp circling the upper ten inches, drawn together to resist the attacks of 1,000 warriors and 100,000 strikes. The enemy provoked me. Old crimson blood turned black with time stared back at me, awaiting my strategy.

I met the challenge and facing the *makiwara*, bowed, and shouted several times, *"Onegai shimasu—gendo-ryoku, onegai shimasu—gendo-ryoku."* This was the verbal preparation for "please teach me" coupled with "to endure with driving force." I fell into a deep measured stance ready to unleash 3,000 punches, followed by 2,000 sword hand strikes, totaling 5,000 in all. Positioning for the battle, I squeezed my fist tightly as the blood quickly forced itself out and then cocked it to my hip. My lead fist extended slowly and deliberately, barely touching the *makiwara* as a gauge for distance. Both swords crossed as if for *tachiojo* (to die standing up).

My eyes fixed themselves on the enemy as I adjusted and angled my stance in anticipation toward the target and cleared my mind. Battle was about to ensue.

Several *kiai*s filled the air— *Eeii! Eeii! Eeii! Eeii!* Then passion let go. With each smashing punch, I expelled the unwanted air and refilled with new explosive *ki,* the vital force bearing life itself. As each blasting punch unleashed from my hip and it made contact with the hemp that encircled the *makiwara,* I let out the sound of a thousand warriors on horseback. With each full knuckle punch I *kiai*d and the sound echoed through the *dojo* as though an army were present and engaged in a full battle.

The war manifested as a cadence of pounding martial arts exactness. Military mind and Zen mind emerged and blended. I dug my feet into the *tatami* as if to be rooted in granite and the Zen mind began to bury itself entranced within the chasm of the *makiwara* soul. The bolts holding the *makiwara* into the concrete stressed with the hammering, but held as they became the bridge between me and a time long forgotten that was the seed of this proud *dojo.*

The Zen of *makiwara* appears comparatively simple to understand but requires a difficult ordeal of discipline to achieve. The practice of *makiwara* must be incredibly deliberate, forever intense, and nothing less. It must continue in a direct, self-reliant, self-denying manner as nature is to life, full of the ascetic spirit that goes well with the fighting spirit and the mind of the stoic *bujin.* The *bujin (samurai* or *Budoka)* needs to maintain an open mind toward life but must be single-minded in battle with one objective: to fight to win, neither looking backward nor sideways. To go straight forward and crush the enemies of the mind and not allow oneself to be encumbered in any way, be it physical, emotional, or intellectual.

Kiai after *kiai* echoed through the caverns of the *Budo* spirit. The *keikojo* vibrated with the sound of a one-man battle. The course of human conflict in the search of martial prowess continued onward. The journey now made its way into the belly of the dragon, as I was deep in mind and spirit. The cadence continued for over an hour as sweat poured off my body. Smashing my armored fist against the *makiwara*, I drew in deeper breaths as if to find a second wind. Steam rose from my chest in the crystal frozen air to meet the cold stillness now sharpening the presence of my being. Twisting and driving each blow home, I finally reached the magic number sought, and upon 3,000 I switched to the blade of the hand, charging full ahead, sharpening the sword.

Without missing a beat, my mind propelled the fighting spirit forward to win. Onward I plummeted into the corners of the universal way, the essence of waging a one-man war. As I shifted my hips in a sharp arc, my sword hand cut through the air with deadening power to find its mark. Onward I drove as if possessed, as one who leads an army of universal mercenaries. The *kiai* now began to contain an almost inhuman cry with even greater magnification. Forward I forced myself and lost consciousness of who I was.

I slammed home a thousand cuts with my hand in an unending fury to conquer my old familiar fears and the enemies that lay before me.

"Once again!" The great Zen shout "Katsu!" thundered as I wheeled my sword to the advancing forces. There, at Shigara, my eyes fixed their gaze across the sea at the break of dawn. The odds were overwhelming in what appeared to be a wave of Mongol warriors advancing for battle. Outnumbered by superior forces, the samurai were shocked to hear the Mongols not only killed the warriors who opposed them, which was to be expected, but also massacred the women and children. This was something the samurai would never do, and this also became the first mistake for the Mongol invaders.

The samurai, instead of waiting for reinforcements from Kamakura, rode out to challenge the bravest Mongols individually. But the Mongols simply opened their doors, then closed the trap as disciplined ranks engulfed each lone samurai. Seasoned samurai wielded swords and halberds, one against many, and cut their way through the masses of bodies that advanced upon their sword. The Mongol losses were great, but the odds were too much and overpowered the samurai. The samurai who rode horses were thrown by their steeds as the unfamiliar sound of kettle drums sent the animals into a frenzy. Nevertheless, the samurai fought fiercely as though the ancient gods themselves rode with them. The Mongols were only able to march a short distance before failing to advance further. A disciplined samurai was indeed the greatest warrior of all.

One samurai against ten or twenty Mongols wheeled his halberd in sweeping, arcing motions. Thrusting, stabbing, and cutting, his spirit controlled his destiny. As the samurai stood upon the bodies of Mongol soldiers, his powerful downward stroke broke the blade of his halberd in two. Now left with only his long sword and short dirk, he spun and cut mercilessly, charging full into the crimson carnage of the enemy. The bloodbath raged in all directions, and the clash of armor (yoroi) against armor rang out. Then the samurai took two arrows in the legs—one to the armor-plated calf, but another slipped through into his thigh.

Another arrow pierced his shoulder guards and sank into flesh as he fought and fell to the ground. Kneeling down, he wheeled in a mass of circular cuts, driving thrusts. There, slicing bone and flesh, and throwing off his kabuto (war helmet), he roared out a cry of ferocious intensity, watched the blood flow from his armor, and looked up to the heavens as the Mongols backed away in fright.

Holding his sword and reaching toward the burning sky amidst the pile of corpses, he yelled to the gods and the Buddhas. Victory came for a glorious moment as he sought the truth of Zen, then found it and upon doing so drove his sword into his abdomen and died honorably.

Fearing a night attack, the Mongols burned the coastal towns they had taken and sailed away. The second wave of the Mongol invasion met a typhoon sent by the gods. A kamikaze, divine wind, ripped through the green seas of Japan and its countryside, where a warrior attack mass of 30,000 prepared its campaign, and destroyed the Mongol fleet. The samurai were saved by the laws of nature and the seishin of the universe.

My sword hand *(tegatana)* felt as though it were on fire, but I drove myself relentlessly to my goal. Slicing through the morning air I surgically stroked each cut with the entire soul to accomplish my mission. Blood flowed into my sword edge with each blast against the *makiwara,* and then began to seep from an old injury in the knuckle. The straw sheath turned crimson red, then soaked deep red as I advanced forward into the dynamic reality of victory and honor. I *kiai*d over and over from the depths of my soul as though to move the very ground I stood upon, and bore down even more. Then at 1,000 I shifted to the opposite side without missing a beat to begin the ritual once more. Now into more than 4,000 strikes, my spirit began to carry me forward.

The opposite striking hand slammed into my hip each time I struck with the other, leaving my *keikogi* bloodstained over my entire waist region. I slipped back and forth into a meditation state, never losing count, only finding more repetitions had lapsed, bringing me closer to the ultimate mark.

No one was there to support me, no one was there to endorse my battle, only the reality that with each breath, each driving blow, I would become victorious in the Spartan way.

How many other *karateka* trainees around the world are doing as I am in this moment, I thought, seeking the higher levels of understanding and perception of life itself. While the average student lay in sleep under the protection of family, unaware that his life could be challenged in a moment, I moved further up the canyon of existence, grasping at each vital moment. I would conquer the enemy within.

An illuminating essence, a shimmer of light began to emerge from a break in the granite wall and became brighter as I moved toward it. It was barely wide enough for a man to squeeze through, but I forced my body into the wall, not knowing what lay beyond. Fear attempted to rip at my mind, but forward I continued to immerse my soul. Howling winds tore at my eyes and hair, countering my desire to win, but stopping was not an option.

Drawing closer to what appeared to be an opening only seven or ten feet away, I inched further, but the passage was too tight. I was so close yet unable to move forward more than perhaps an inch at a time. My muscles strained to continue, but with each grueling instant I faced fear of being stuck in time forever.

Then, as the gods allowed, I managed to gain some distance, and hope raced through my heart and veins. Now I was only a foot from the opening ahead. I reached my arm and hand out, while cold stone tore into my chest and back. Reaching ever so much, stretching with all my will, I could barely grab the edge of the outer opening that lay only inches in front of me. Muscles began to labor but my will became stronger, pressing me onward. The quest of enlightenment now remained within my dimension.

Some stones began to give way and I felt myself move forward as I shifted my legs. Part of me felt as if I were being ripped limb from limb, while the other part felt great compassion and love sweeping my body in waves of eternal emotion. The intensity of the distant essence now touched my face and shoulder as I began to move out of the crushing gap. Intense light warmed my being and my existence of mind, body, and spirit. The stream of energy gave me new life, as I broke completely through to the other side in one final effort. There standing in front of me, calm and serene, asking for nothing, was the mirror image of myself at total peace, as one who has found his place in the universe.

The reality and the finding were now clear. I was to go onward to seek higher goals, to unfathomable depths of the human heart, and to serve by example only to manifest the way. This was the *do*—the way—of *Budo*.

Four thousand. I stopped and stood witness to the task that now lay behind me and in testimony of *truly getting it*.

My hands were swollen and in several places blood flowed from minor wounds. My body was drenched with sweat and my uniform dripped onto the *tatami* the life force that came from my enduring journey. I dropped to my knees and looked at the clock upon the wall; more than two hours had passed. I felt no pain, no loss, only the awakening and continual presence of my victorious realization. Steam rolled up from my body as I meditated. I knew that for one moment in time, one solitary instant with the sweaty taste of honor,

I built the bridge that connected the vast here-now with the final destiny of my own soul. I touched the face of Universal Life. This was the *makiwara* of diligence, the inexhaustible struggle for honorable intent based on enlightenment *(satori)*.

It seemed the vestige of icons past stood in tranquility circling my presence in a watchful state, acknowledging what I had experienced. It is for only those brief moments that the conquerors of the human heart ever experience the immovable mind in its instant of triumph. The shadows that had appeared now disappeared just as quickly.

I returned somehow elated above the previous state I experienced and removed myself from the *taijo* and my *misogi-renshu* (purification training). The *makiwara* had first been the enemy, the grueling opposition in the battle to find my true self, and then the ominous tide did what nature intended it to do. It shifted in a different direction and soon the transformation was made to seize each invaluable moment. I diligently scaled the granite chasm to become the champion of the human heart.

The *dojo* now lay silent as the morning sun began to glisten through the *idiguchi* as it rose in the east of the morning freeze. Casting an orange glow through the doorway glass, the sun's warmth flowed inward like water in a stream. The snow outside cast a brilliant reflection to the heavens and would soon melt the condensation and ice formed on the glass overnight.

A great sensation fell over me as I cleared a small hole in the frostly glass with my fist and peered outside, knowing I victoriously won the challenge of discipline over the long night of *seishin tanren* (spirit-forging). Few students would even hear of this practice over the years, as humility and honor quite often held my excitement back. Many wondered how to achieve greatness or how I became so proficient in the way of *karate-do,* assuming that a weekly schedule of practice and numerous fighting engagements were merely enough. Not true, the real battle of becoming the best was to cultivate a heart of honor and a sterling character in the constant search for the most clear truth. Most of all, you never allow yourself to settle for second place.

This was the true meaning of *ryomi*— reflection — to go beyond.

Turning to walk toward the locker room, I thought of the countless warriors who would enter the *dojo* later that day to take cadence from the instructor who would lead them, and I knew I would feel my strongest. Their spirit and the act of winning drove my spirit onward with purpose and forced me to dig even deeper into the ways of life and my very own purpose. Just what was the lesson I needed to learn? Our practice was never perfect but still we strove for perfect practice, and no matter how much one tries, he still is flawed, incomplete in some way, but perfect in others.

I passed the *makiwara* and stopping there I noticed the mats covered with puddles of sweat, the by-product of *Budo* fortitude and the human spirit. The *makiwara* hemp was damp, now soft with the blood and sweat measured in hammering thrusts by the thousands. Soon the crimson would turn dark red, then blacken and become hard for the next ordeal upon its sheath. Anyone coming in for practice would hardly make note of the difference. Only those *bujin* who press themselves onward like war horses to execute more *makiwara* will realize the destiny apparent from last night's trial of the human spirit.

I sighed briefly, looked the *taijo* over, and thought to myself, *Oh well, better get going, I've got training to do this afternoon and more makiwara.*

"Gendo-ryoku no Bujin"— The driving force of the fighting man.

Nintai— Perseverance

CHAPTER SIX

Gasping for Air!
The Battle in the Furnace

The small *machi dojo* (inner-city training *dojo)*, was in sight. Pulling my rusty car into the alley, I dodged garbage cans and cast-off furniture getting to the back of the *dojo*. Rows of various-size garages lined the back alley, positioned behind houses built in the 1930s and 40s. Most cast a color of dreary brown or blue-grey. The one-and-a-half-car garage I was looking for was old but built with the strength of a fortress. I could see it midway down the alley's obstacle course. So I carefully drove to the back of the makeshift training facility and parked my car.

It was a midsummer day but I remembered training here in the dead of winter, months earlier. The wet snow was piled high upon the rooftops and in the streets. One could glance at many of the mirror-image homes during the intense morning frost to see the chimneys pumping grey, hot smoke into the freezing morning air. Not even the slightest wind blew on those days. The frost sitting on my window, my auto heater fruitlessly blowing full blast, foretold what was in store for me. I remember how I struggled through the snow and how it crunched under my feet as I forced my way to the *dojo* door. Dogs didn't even venture out and brave the cold on those mornings.

I thanked my lucky stars that today I would not have to endure the despicable temperature biting at my body in the dead of winter. It would drop below freezing without a heater in the *dojo*. Our heat source was the intense use of our bodies in motion as a means to warm the surroundings of the war zone and our souls. *God,* I asked from time to time, *how can I possibly go on?* But each day came and went, each difficult challenge was painfully dealt with, and I survived the ritual of punishment the ancient *Budo*-way.

I entered the backyard and walked toward the *dojo* to see Sensei waiting for a handful of students. We were a small group in those days, set on forging our destiny in the ways of battle as tough street-fighters with high-spirited expectations. *"Osu!"* I shouted and bowed as Sensei responded. I was always aware of his moods and could readily see if his intentions for the practice session would result in a deadly severe experience or one of lesser brutality. We wanted to find him in a good mood. He said, "Jack-*san,* change into your *keikogi* and start your *taiso.* It's going to be a flaming morning." I looked over my shoulder to see the summer sun creeping up over the roof, which meant the *dojo* temperature was sure to reach the 100-degree mark later. The thing you dreaded most was about to arrive—heat.

We started practice in early morning to evade the intensity that nature provided us, but most times we didn't finish until late. By then, exhaustion from enduring the humid heat dropped us to our knees.

I entered the *dojo* to see three familiar faces and one new man. You made friends slowly in the *dojo,* as few stayed for very long. But over time, adversity seemed to bond everyone who remained to endure. As in any gathering, formalities were strict, but during the hard practices, many tempers slipped, allowing emotions to get out of control and producing angry results. Through blood and sweat, bonds *(kizuna)* became tightened and commitments were reconfirmed. It was simple—you dealt with the anguish or you quit. We would lose a newcomer each week and then pick up occasional new blood who would stay until broken under the pressure. Your will to survive and become the best had to override your fears and discouragement. You acknowledged no room for excuses, as Sensei did not countenance any. This practice was for those who could endure the mental and physical pain. Those with the temperament to achieve ultimate mastery over any weakness to attain great honor were the survivors.

Stepping into the *dojo,* one would see that all the interior walls had been covered with three-quarter-inch hard plywood rising seven feet to the ceiling, where it met the old timber rafters. The top of the room was dark, since the overhead lights hung low as if to focus on those standing in readiness beneath. The floor was covered, not with the *tatami* I now have come to use, but with hard plywood. In simple terms, the *dojo* became a square chasm of wall-to-wall intensity with no ventilation—a cube with no more than the still presence of your pounding heart and those breathing hard around you.

In time, you would be desperate, seeking freedom from the hot humid air, grasping to find sanity during the hard moment of truth. You learned to desperately search for the inner courage to find *satori* (enlightenment). Some of us did from time to time, and in that sweet space between life and death—known as *yuyo* for the *samurai*—each warrior gained that special insight. In a flash it was there, then in the next moment it was gone like some sacred secret you held in the palm of your hand only to have it stolen away.

The vital key was to hang on, to hold fast and hope the mind-enhancing wisdom that came to the lucky ones came to you before your guts felt as if they were going to break loose, twist, and cramp in battle. We all sought those fleeting enigmas to be our own. Describing their meaning was impossible; achieving their mysteries even more so. I suppose you could describe it as seeing the light and then moving through it to the other side where special wisdom was realized. The enrichment of these principles was the priceless gem only understood by the owner, the one who died and returned. This was the real *Budo* of old.

We all found a place to pay homage to our system and our guide. Meditating, I knew the challenge that lay before me. I sat in *seiza,* as a *samurai* preparing for battle, chanting life-giving and life-taking prayers.

I could hear a locust outside begin to sing as the sizzling sun drew a line of intense white light through the door. At least Sensei didn't close the door! I had no more than loosened up my *karate* bones in brief, stretched only a few minutes, when sweat ran down my forehead as I focused on my breathing. The wooden floor would run red with blood today. I could feel it. I could see old black marks everywhere, from old and recent injuries that left crimson clues on the floor as a reminder of days past and battles fought.

Sensei shouted, *"Yame!"* (Stop!) We opened our eyes, stood up, and waited for our mentor to give us the commands. He then yelled, "First we'll warm up with some *kihon* [basics], then *kumite* [free-sparring]." On command we fell into our fighting stances to begin the ritual of repetition in striking, blocking, and kicking techniques. This redundant ritual solidified the movements in harmony with nature. They tempered the skill needed to attack and win against the enemy. My *keikogi* filled with sweat quickly. Sensei shouted, *" Tsuyoi, tsuyoi!* [Harder!] Do not hold back, men—*we live to die!"* as we stepped up the pace.

The race for the ultimate level of excellence had begun. Sensei drove us as Spartans on the battlefield, and we accepted the punishment in the solitude of a private enclave which would master our minds. Under a mask of stoicism, we controlled our emotions, even though the fear, frustration, and anger kept pushing to come out and force a breakdown. The capacity to bear pain leads one to uncharted levels of personal dominance in a world filled with doubt and confusion. This was certain. We had to win!

As my spirits stayed strong, I remembered the saying, *"Taorete nochi yamu"*—Fight to the last or stop only after you have been struck down. This Japanese saying exemplifies the courage of the warrior who wouldn't stop until he was incapable of battling further.

The air began to turn stale and with it our struggle to gain fresh oxygen increased greatly. Exhaustion came and went in waves of endurance. Next a series of basic kicks was practiced, each with the energy to do physical harm. Not one of us wavered in our determination to continue. As lightning kicks flew through the air, our *kiai*s dominated the morning silence like the first crack of thunder during a summer's storm, moments before the downpour. The *dojo* took on a new essence as though the ancient *Budoka* were watching us perform. It was as if Itosu, Yasutsune Sensei, known as Iron Horse from his ability to absorb strikes from opponents, were looking down upon us. Itosu Sensei was the founder of the *Shudokan* system of *karate*.

I knew there were other greats as well, too numerous to mention, and recalled short visions of great warrior stories as told by my teacher. Aggressively, we pushed forward.

"Matte, Matte!" (Stop!), shouted Sensei. "Take five minutes and tape your hands and weak points." I knew this could only mean one thing—*kumite* was about to begin. We bowed and rushed outside to catch our breath of fresh air, but it was short-lived as Sensei demanded our speedy readiness and soon forced us back into the lion's den. The gravity of full contact and full battle readiness was before me, as was the heat. We wore no padding for safety back then. No extra high-tech protection was allowed, with exception of taping old injuries in need of reinforcement.

True warfare in the streets meant you were to be prepared to the max, and my teacher was one who discouraged the modern-day flashy equipment available on the martial arts market. "No time for pads in the streets, no time for pads in the *dojo*," Sensei would say. I understood this to be true over time with a battle-subjected mind. Besides, as one's body learns to absorb the powerful *karate* blows, it solidifies, tempers, and learns to resist many attacks. One learns to give, slip, absorb, and evade to become resilient in mind and body. And so we did. We learned well to value life, to live to die.

Intense practice and difficult training spread over several days developed the extreme inexhaustible spirit *(fudoshin)*. This type of practice was done for the ultimate purpose of *misogi*, purification. The general term is *shugyo* (austerity training) or maximum training practice. There are stories of great masters of *Aiki-Budo* who performed *shugyo*. One was Ueshiba Sensei who searched his entire life for the perfection of character in his pilgrimage to higher learning.

Ueshiba Sensei would invite several of his star pupils to a retreat in Kyoto for twenty or more days. This type of practice allowed the student to focus total energy, mind and body, on development. A special area hidden halfway up the mountain was far from the city and secluded for intense practice. In fact, this area was where the great swordmaster and general Yoshitsune was said to have done his austerity training. Ueshiba Sensei would often wake his students unexpectedly in the middle of the night and direct them to prepare for special practice.

Up the mountain they would go in pitch darkness, no lights or moon to guide them. Ueshiba Sensei moved quickly up trails and ledges while others followed, attempting to stay close behind.

Once on top of the hill, all secured their *hachi-maki* (headbands) and drew real *katana* (swords). They took turns in total darkness attacking Ueshiba Sensei from various postures and positions. "This is called *ki* training," said Ueshiba Sensei. The great *aikido sensei* changed roles and became attacker next, using great accuracy and control during the practice. Students said they could see the flash of the sword come close to their white *hachi-maki,* then stop in an instant. This was termed "sword wind," and one could feel it faintly.

Food was minimal, like pickled radish and rice gruel for nourishment. The gathering of mountain herbs offered other specialties not found at lower altitudes and sustained the vigil.

This story from the *aikido* master Gozo Shioda Sensei reminded me of the type of practice I felt was now upon me—an experience long to remember. I often wondered whether others trained in this method, but later learned I was fortunate to be one of the few who truly experienced this formidable revelation, while others could only dream of it. This was the way. No shortcut method or fantasy in "book form" to muddy and dilute my thinking was acceptable. It was real, it was alive. Too many others had too often spoken of the rituals of austerity as though they themselves actually partook in them, only to reveal knowledge never experienced on a personal level. Secondhand stories from teachers who never walked the battle line would not be a measure of my life.

The battle was upon us. Shins wrapped, wrists and injured knuckles taped, we moved into the arena. There was Dave, Dan, Kevin, and me. Each one of us from different lifestyles and backgrounds came to find respect among each other that sizzling day. Dan was stocky, tough, and experienced from earlier practice with Sensei. Kevin was lean and quick, and Dave was heavier, stronger, and slow. I, well, I was crazy. I wanted to move around these guys like the wind, strike from nowhere but everywhere. I enjoyed trapping my man in a corner and driving him to the earth.

The earlier days on concrete and steel floors had solidified my demand for victory and now made this floor of plywood seem soft and ready for ultimate battle triumph. Those days of victory were not always mine, and I would learn I wasn't always the toughest.

I paired off with Dave, with whom I was acquainted from an earlier school in which we both trained. It was most unfortunate that this other *dojo* was regarded as one where talk was really the walk. He, like I, became frustrated at the hypocritical nonsense and hairbrain antics based on phony certification. We saw the light early on. Disillusioned at first and highly frustrated later, I felt honored to have been accepted into my current *sensei's* real world of *Budo*. Both Dave and I gravitated to what could be called the *Shinken Shobu Dojo* (Duel with Live Blades *Dojo*). Actually, the *dojo* was called *Senso to Heiwa Dojo* (War and Peace *Dojo*).

Sensei shouted, *"Renzoku kumite!"* (give-and-take free-sparring). The *dojo* could not have been more than twelve by fifteen feet in size. We faced our partners and bowed as our minds began to gain a warrior state of emotion. Both two-man groups would attack in a straight line back and forth, smashing against the walls as they stopped our momentum. One side would attack and the other could only defend and counter. Countering an attack was an art in itself, but Sensei had taught us to launch our assaults as though a driving storm were in our hearts.

On his command, we began. *"Hajime!"* he screamed. Thundering legs and arms flew. Fists followed by sweat spun off in all directions. I attacked with combinations, first multiple hand attacks and then foot sweeps to finish my *aite*. Dave returned the volley to find his mark against my ribs and chest. My shins crashed against his forearms, and my foot sunk deep into his stomach. Down he went and back up again. We collided with Kevin and Dan as they moved in unison with us at the commands Sensei rang out warning us not to hesitate. I sucked wind to catch my breath, then saw Sensei smash Dan once with his reverse punch to reprimand his lack of spirit. Dan bounced back with fury. Wave after wave of attacks and defensive maneuvering went on for over a grueling hour. Exhaustion was setting in as the temperature reached the upper nineties. I knew the mercury would soar well over the 100-degree mark today since August was the most difficult month to practice in the Midwest.

Sensei shouted, *"Matte!"* We all stopped to catch our breath. "Everyone, down and give me 100 push-ups." Grinding through these were a break in the battle, so I sucked in my breath deeply as I attempted to finish the set. I noticed out of the corner of my eye the other boys failing to meet Sensei's demands, as was I, but still I forged onward. Sensei stopped us and motioned for us to go outside and breathe for five minutes. He announced we were to fight against the wooden wall next. "Battle against the hard wall, *samurai!*" he shouted. This meant we would pair off in a corner and, moving from one wall to the other, absorb blows, block offensive tactics, and grapple to the ground as if in a deadly battle. No running backward, only the resolve to stand your ground and do battle. You could dodge, create evasive action, evade to the left and right, duck and slip, or worse yet, take the blows dying under the impact and losing face. It was a test of Spartan willpower, a conditioning of the spirit.

I sat outside the *dojo* door. Looking over my shoulder, I peered in to see the wooden floor was now wet from sweat and blood smeared here and there from a cut above one of the boy's eyes. Sensei mentioned it wasn't bad and should be taped and butterflied after the session was over. As the saying went, "If you could still move, you were well enough to continue." I threw some water on my face from a bucket that stood outside. Looking up, I could see storm clouds beginning to form high in the sky.

A few of the neighborhood kids hung close to the fence watching me and taking it all in, as if thinking these *karateka* must be out of their minds. I wondered whether my car was still intact in the alley. Were the wheels or stereo snatched from my heap? I then drifted back to my quest. The sun disappeared behind a dark cloud, bringing relief from the direct brightness, but the humidity bore down. Some distant thunder, now beginning to grow closer, sounded off as if to remind me that the Great *Budo* was watching the turn of events. Weather changes quickly in the Midwest. The center of the storm was approaching us all.

"Ikimassho," (Let's go) Sensei grunted.

Back into the *dojo* we went, but with a different attitude this time, as if to say, "let's get it on." The intensity and humid air hit me in the face upon my entrance. Tired and weary, we were all nonetheless ready to take on the challenge of the wooden wall. Pairing off with Dan this time, I stood with my back to one corner, while Dave found another corner and paired off with Kevin. Sensei shouted, "Anyone who stops will find themselves doing *kumite* with me. Is that understood?" We all shouted back, "*Hai,* Sensei, *wakarimasu.*" (We understand.) Standing motionless, my eyes were fixed on Dan. We were friends, partners on the path to enlightenment, but now our journey changed to battle strategy, and our quest became that of individual survival in warfare.

My elbow stung from a kick, my head throbbed from a hook, and my ankle was slightly swollen from an unsuccessful sweep attempt, but I readied my *seishin* (spirit). Again, behind another roll of thunder, Sensei rang out, *"Hajime!"* Dan moved from side to side to set me up. Quarters were tight and I noticed blood running down his face from his eye wound. I taunted him, distracted his mind by tapping his leg with my own in an attempt to frustrate any means of level strategy. He charged with an inside front kick to my chest. I side-moved and countered with a reverse punch, but too late, he caught me with his sword strike to the shoulder. I quickly moved back to my corner and again he attacked. This time he attempted to sweep my forward leg full power. I snatched it upward as his powerful leg swept under mine. The momentum threw him off balance, and I countered with a hook to the body, then the head. My body blow connected with its mark, but my head shot missed. My fist sunk deep into his solar plexus and down he went. Sensei yelled, "Get up, let's get this show moving. Now!" I reached down to help Dan up, but he pulled away and rose on his own, no doubt angered. Sensei screamed, "Harder, harder, push, push!" And so we did. The pace was picking up, the spirits were stretched to the limit, and the heat poured on. I drove onward.

Another attack, and this time a series of roundhouse kicks flew in. My movement was hindered because of the walls, so I covered and took the first blast, then felt the other one riddle my thigh, then another came into my ribs. I blocked and trapped this one. In one massive show of strength, I swept his other leg and down we both went. Banging against the wall, we flew to the floor. Dan launched a punch at me with a powerful fist as we went down, connecting with the back of my head. My brain spun, but not in vain. Dan hit the floor with his back, too absorbed with his last hook punch while going down, and didn't break his fall. Bad move! The wind blew out of him like a candle as he made contact and now lay against the wood. He gasped for air, and Sensei stopped the battle.

"*Matte,* everyone, catch your wind and change positions—*kawaru.*" Dan began to gain his senses and I pulled him up. More submissive to my skill, he accepted my help and stood up. On this round, he moved to the defensive position and I became the aggressor, the attacker. Now I was to become the windstorm, the lightning out of the sky, and the driving rain in the night. As my thoughts passed through my mind, the rain began to pour outside. The whole group exhibited pure exhaustion and continuing onward was a complete labor of the spirit. My guts began to tighten and wrench under the pressure, as if I was hit mid-level repeatedly. I knew I had only minutes left before I too would find myself on the deck holding myself together, gasping for any drop of oxygen accessible in the stifling hot summer air.

I wanted so to see the enlightenment that I sought in these profoundly intense workouts, a glimmer of the universal magic that transpires every ounce of your being when found. Where was my *ki?*

Dave raced for the *dojo* door and running into the yard lost his morning meal and his need to light up for a cigarette. His gut-wrenching ordeal came to a natural end, in dishonor. Down on all fours in the still solitude of the driving rain he remained. Kevin was left alone now, faltering against the back partition. Sensei shouted, "Kevin, begin *makiwara* until you finish 500 repetitions." Grinding out the difficult words, Kevin answered, "*Hai,* Sensei, *wakarimasu.*" He began to pound away.

Now the rhythm of *makiwara* would accompany my last stand. I gathered my inner strength and waited for the command. *"Hajime,"* said Sensei. Almost falling over each other, we collided on my first assault. The slam of Dan's heavy body against the wooden wall shook the building like so many other times. I grabbed his *keikogi* with my left hand while pressing him against the wall and let loose three or four right-hand punches or hooks. My wind was at a loss and my focus was now uncentered. I was ready to drop to my knees when I heard Sensei holler, "In *Budo,* you die before you lose."

I backed off my opponent, then feeling as though new energy found my soul, I *kiai*d and attacked fearlessly in a final attempt to find the light.

The wind was behind me, the charge had ignited an uncontrollable but calculating firestorm. I attacked! Front kicks, roundhouse kicks found their marks. I forced my light weight against his and seemed to drive him forcibly into the wood. My elbow let go and found home against his solar plexus. *Again! Power! Power!* I kept saying to myself. In a desperate attempt, Dan brought his knee up to meet my groin but I sidestepped to catch his leg as he brought it up and slammed him once again to the floor. One of his reverse punches caught my cheek as I straddled his side. Grappling, I found myself behind him, wrapped my arm around his neck, and began to choke him out. It didn't work and he broke away.

We both struggled to our feet. Pushing, he slammed me between the wall and his brute force. I held on and Sensei shouted, *"Matte!"* Sensei hollered the same words several times before I released him. He fell to the floor, but I stood my ground at attention waiting for the next command. For the first time in the session, I felt connected, then Sensei said, "Relax, Jack-*san,* and go outside to catch your wind." I gave Dan a tug. He looked at me submissively and said, "*Domo,* Jack."

The cloudburst had blown itself out then passed and the battle was over. Sensei called to Kevin to stop his *makiwara*. All of us fell to the ground to find new strength in relief. The ordeal was over. All of us on our knees and backs. I shifted my eyes to the others gasping for vital energy and life to sustain themselves. No anger, no hostilities, and no regrets—we conquered our own fears. The sun now returned, the birds began to sing, and my heart felt good. We found a piece of the great spirit of *Budo* and bonded as brothers for many moments during our conflict. It was this type of practice that made men out of boys. The unrelenting demands of Sensei and the total obsession to win against one's weak side had become a triumphant victory for individual honor. I wanted so much to be like my Sensei, to be as honorable and as stoic as he. I knew that I would become the guide and *sensei* someday.

I knew I could become a leader of men, if I didn't die first. But then, that was the key. That was the secret I longed to find. There it was in front of me. I know what the *samurai* sought, "to live is to die, to encourage death and accept it openly as life itself."

No fear of death; no fear of failure. I smiled to myself and reentered the *dojo* for clean-up. *Budo* had showed me something I couldn't buy in any way. For one special, brief moment in time, once again I found a shimmer of *satori*.

Giri—Obligation

CHAPTER SEVEN

Facing the Mountain: The Ordeal of Sanchin Kata

I took the ultimate in physical abuse seeking the door to the other side: receiving brutal strikes to my torso, having wood shattered over every conceivable part of my body and concrete cinderblocks smashed down upon my head. Warrior arrows were set against various parts of my body and forced against skin and muscle while I flexed them to their breaking point.

Sanchin, the *kata* of perseverance and fortitude, has tested my total being in the reality of harmonizing my pain threshold with my mind. *Kata,* or forms practice, compromises some of the most ancient methods of personal development without the use of actual combat. They allow one or more *bujin* to stage battle without actually acknowledging the unmerciful engagement of warfare. Historically, some *kata* have been very violent, and contact was made on controlled levels to allow one to deal with pain and fortitude. From several moves dealing with attacks, defenses, and counterattacks to hundreds of complicated variations in grappling, choking, and joint locking, *kata* were conceived and rallied in all different casts and configurations.

One day I received a letter from my teacher about a new challenge I would meet under some strange circumstances. I quote: "Jack-*san,* your presence is required at my home for the administration of one of the oldest forms of *karate-do kata,* the *Sanchin.* It will require a persevering attitude and the heart of the heavens to endure. Be at my home no later than 7:00 AM on Saturday and bring fifty clean and cut pine boards measuring one by twelve inches cut into nine-inch lengths. I will supply the rest of the materials such as concrete slabs, bricks, and arrows. Don't worry, *shimpai nai,* your journey will bring forth much reward. Do not be late!"

As I sat in my solitude, thunder roared near my house. Since I lived on a lake, I could watch the storms approaching from the west. A sheet of rain in a downpour hit the window. It seemed to cause a premonition deep within me of what was to come as I opened and read the intense words of Sensei's letter. A new form of education was about to unfold. Although excited about this quest, I shuddered at the consequences I might endure if I didn't perform under pressure.

The rain seemed to come down even harder that moment, putting an edge on my temperament. *Sanchin kata* means "three battles" or "three points," and contains the challenge and understanding of the mind, body, and spirit. It tests one's personal strength of inner *ki* and deals with the phenomenon of mysterious Oriental breathing techniques or *kokyu-ho.* The classical *Budo* forms or *kata* were used as vehicles to master *seishin tanren* (spirit-forging) and they are grueling in their puritanical nature. The tremendous will power and consistency necessary to pursue this type of practice bestow a realization of the moral and physical meaning of life itself.

This *kata* is the moral fiber that left *Budoka* in awe of their indomitable dynamic power. It produces something special when executed correctly over years. *Sanchin* is one of the most ancient *kata* and goes back to the teachings of the great *karate* master, Higashiona, Kanryo—founder of the *Naha-te* system. The deep-rooted stance and dynamic contraction of the muscles combined with mysterious breathing allow the practitioner to become mentally resistant to punishment and pain of various degree. The *kata* builds fortitude and self-realization from its tenacious practice when performed in a dedicated manner.

I had seen this *kata* practiced in the past by many martial artists, but it wasn't until that grey, rainy, stormy day that I truly found the metal steel of *sanchin* as expressed by my teacher. As one performs this *kata,* the enraptured technician expresses the resounding exhalation of forceful breathing in a slow-motion dance based on concrete unity that seems to blend with the universal authority.

Light and dark become one, positive and negative meet in sheer harmony as the true acknowledgment and wonders of mastery unfold. The expression becomes the *yin* and *yang* of life. A tranquil essence based on phenomenal self-control emphasizes the ultimate strength of the martial artist in a most beautiful state. Mind and body climb to the ultimate acme of oneness, and the nature of *Budo* unfolds clearly for the practitioner.

Sanchin, it is found, teaches one that through practice the "physical hardship will forge the fighting spirit shaping a predetermined destiny, and the spiritual practice will perfect the techniques." So it is through this *sanchin* practice that I became awakened by the forces of the universe.

Driving through the urban Detroit area where my teacher lived, I rounded the corner onto his street. Stopping, I noticed the remains of what seemed to have been a war overnight. I encroached slowly up the boulevard in my chunky old Camaro, passing one auto without wheels, completely stripped sitting on its axle and springs, another one turned over by who knows what, and a third slammed sideways into a porch. Several shady individuals walked the streets in search of no good, I was sure. In the distance I could see Sensei's house and drove slowly up to it and parked at the curb. Driveways were in the back of these inner-city dwellings next to old-fashioned one-car garages. I locked my door and laughed to myself, wondering what the point was, and trekked up to my teacher's front door. In the distance down the road I could see smoke rising from another house or structure on fire. If you were to wake up here on the doorstep, I believe you could get the instant impression of being in the center of the war-torn city of Beirut, Lebanon.

I rang the bell, but no answer. I rang it again, but still no answer. Knocking louder on the door, I listened for a stirring in the house. Sensei lived upstairs and kept late hours, so I imagined he would have stayed up for this session soon to begin. Then I heard some fumbling and a turn of a lock, the release of a deadbolt, and the removal of an iron rod held against the inside of the door. Strange as it may seem, no one was going to get in without a battle or, as a matter of argument, get out easily. Opening the old oak door was Sensei. His disgruntled look from some weary all-night vigil was offset by a calm welcome to his residence, or as he called it, "the war room."

"Jack-*san*, please, *dozo, dozo,* come up to my *uchi*." Then Sensei relocked a couple of deadbolts back in place. As I mentioned, Sensei lived upstairs; another *katana* (sword) and gun-collecting friend lived on the bottom level. I briefly thought of the arsenal available to repel any assault that may occur in the dark hours of the night. Break-ins, muggings, rapes, and various other crimes were nothing new to the residents of this inner-city neighborhood. A warlike way of life was the norm in a state of confusion and conflict.

So, following him to the top, not knowing what lay ahead for me, I trailed with my *keikogi* in hand. Sensei asked, "Jack-*san,* did you bring all the materials I asked for?"

I answered, "Yes, *Hai,* Sensei," and continued to follow him up. A few photos hung on the walls of the stairwell of *karateka* from various stages of his life, along with memories of martial arts demonstrations.

The old house was typical of those of the late 1940s to early 1950s, with small rooms and thick walls. This one seemed to be more fortified and secure than usual, or so I imagined with warfare on my mind. Entering the top floor, I found an average-size living space. Spread out in a systematic way were hundreds of books, written in everything from English to Japanese, French, and Spanish. I had never seen so many martial arts books in my life, covering everything imaginable from technique, or *waza,* to the intricate healing of battle-induced injuries. My mind danced about the unlimited knowledge conceived in the vast library of icons past, and so I stood motionless while my eyes gazed as though they were a tracking device over each and every binding.

Sensei told me, "*Dozo,* Jack-*san,* look over all my *hon* [books] while I change into something appropriate for your lesson. Watch the older *hon,* they are very delicate."

I answered, "*Hai,* Sensei." Touching what I felt was magical and historically invaluable, I slid my hands over the rare bindings of several texts and pulled an old clothbound book off the shelf. It was faded and smelled of old leaves. I carefully separated the ancient pages. This one no doubt held keys to the life and means of masters only a few ever knew of in times long gone.

Much of the old knowledge was never printed, let alone written down in one's own hand. I opened each page carefully to notice the words describing ancient *jujitsu* as taught by an individual from Kyoto, if I remember correctly. Books on health, healing, choking, vital striking anatomy, and bonesetting were all there. Traditional Japanese earthy colors were used on the covers as well as the more modern printing found in later editions of contemporary martial artists. I found myself in a daze, feeling consumed by the very thing I came to learn about, oblivious to anything around me for the moment. This was a door to the ultimate mysteries of martial prowess out of the past as well as a window to the future for me.

"Jack-*san*," Sensei shouted, "wake up and change into your *keikogi*. We have work to do." Carefully replacing several of the books I had pulled off the shelf, I replied in swift etiquette, "*Hai,* Sensei." Quickly stepping into another room, I changed into my *keikogi*. Practice was about to begin. It would be here that I would learn many new things of a unique *Budo* nature over the months and years to come.

This was the old way, in the teacher's home under the watchful eyes of the master technician. Returning once again, Sensei had me stretch and warm up with *taiso* and then meditate for a brief period before he began his instruction. I gazed over the rest of the room to see *Nippon-to* (Japanese swords) slung across a sword rack. They looked ancient and very special. It was later that Sensei spoke to me of their background and disassembled the "furniture" as it was called, of a sword and instructed me on the art of swordmaking. Shifting my eyes to another object, I looked upon a *kabuto,* or *samurai* helmet, sitting on an Oriental silk cushion. It displayed all the intricate designs commonly expressed in the Japanese *samurai yoroi* (battle armor). Different metals and finishes of various colors and textures were infused into its archaic design.

Sensei said, "Jack-*san,* go down into your car and bring in the extra materials I had you gather." Racing down the stairs, I flew to the door, released the locks, then lunged to the car. I opened my car trunk, grabbed as many of the breaking materials as I could in four alternate trips, and placed them all in their respective places as Sensei instructed me to on the floor in his room. I was startled to see various other materials of a construction nature also gathered on the floor while I was down in my car. I was sure he had other ideas not yet disclosed. I knew that a war on the unstoppable mind and the invincible body was about to begin.

My mind drifted as I sat in a corner.

The samurai warlord from the fighting island of Shikoku, the fiercest, with his 8,000 warriors and generals standing behind him, knew that his challenge would be met. It was the only final way he could convince the enemy of his power and his ultimate supremacy of the lands, so it was now that both warlords would fight shinken shobu—to the death in a single duel with swords and lances.

Rising from their observation perch after agreeing to do battle, both magnificent samurai mounted their proud steeds standing high on opposite knolls, grabbed lances from their samurai retainers, and slowly made their way down the green, grassy valley. Zigzagging back and forth, moving proudly and slowly, each wound his way to the bottom.

The winds blew across the wild valley as the violet wildflowers swayed back and forth like a sea of rolling waves beneath the stallions' hooves. Both forces had gathered at opposite sides of the Shukoku Plain, high above on ridges, and now stood motionless waiting and watching as their generals rode down the gorge to engage in individual mortal combat.

Both samurai knew the consequences if they failed and both had to empty their minds, kill selfish desires, and bravely face their ultimate fate. Many of the samurai who stood silently behind them had rifles and could easily fire on the opponent, but honor held them fast and matchlocks were kept still.

General Saigo was the first to reach the bottom, dressed in his black lacquer-colored yoroi with gold crests upon his breastplate and his short and long swords slung across his belly. Riding a black steed, he seemed invincible as he strode to a place beside a fast-running river. His black armor plates covered his shoulders, arms, and legs. Beautiful dark green tassels hung from the horse's bit, matching the stained green saddle. Both man and beast pumped themselves up for the battle yet to ensue which would determine the fate of almost 20,000 seasoned samurai. Saigo seemed to glide in the saddle high on his horse, his lance held level with the earth, poised to cut that which came before it. His chest was large within the armor. His ancient helmet, kabuto, was beyond description, with sea-green lacquer ornamentation showing a ferocious configuration. Stallion and warrior were as one.

General Kamura slowly and pragmatically descended on the opposite side of the river as Saigo reached the bottom first. He moved ever so slowly, as if to test the other general's temperament and patience. Kamura's armor was bright red, and his breastplate and armor flew the colors of the kiri go san (the paulonia leaf). Clad in the striking crimson colors, his steed was equally bedecked with elaborate materials, finely sewn fighting armor, and brilliant red tassels. The contrast was striking as he rode his white stallion with nostrils flaring, head held high, and long mane flowing with the wind as both prepared for the conflict.

During each warring night, warriors wrote poems, spoke of the next battle, and drank sake in their camps to ease the pain. Blazing fires raged a glow upon high tripod metal stands separating one fighting group of samurai, perhaps lancers, from another group of bow-and-arrow warriors. Each had their specialty, each had their combative place. All of this created an eerie sensation from the distant mountain, as though stars danced on the surface of the earth glowing in the night wind.

They spoke of great past battles, of adventurous campaigns, and listened to the Satsuma flute play softly in the dense, dark, humid air. The sounds drifted through each camp as if a prelude to the fate that awaited each human spirit. As the torches burned, all warriors sat in compliance with the gods, waiting for the jaws of conflict to tighten upon them. Waiting was always the difficult part. Not knowing their fate, they wrote death poems and watched the kenbu, the ancient sword dance performed by professional bujin.

The Imperial troops, with war on their minds and swift expertise in their martial manner, meditated on their belief that they alone would be victorious. It was karma.

Both samurai commanders stood fast, eyes now fixed on each other as they stood on opposite banks of the river that cut the valley in two. As the two exchanged honorable threats as though poetic verses rang out, their stallions pranced, pawing the ground impatiently. General Saigo, in his final words, shouted, "You will not win, the gods are with my destiny."

General Kamura answered, "The gods will determine your fate at the end of my sword, Saigo."

"Let us begin. Our samurai are watching us and we should not hesitate."

With a roar, their horses bolted and charged through the river at full speed. Water sprayed to all sides as the hooves smashed through the blue foaming torrent. As they met in the center, Kamura's lance clipped Saigo's shoulder plate and broke.

On the first pass, a volley of strength met strength. Both battled and exchanged, then the two warriors gained the riverbank as Kamura threw his lance to the ground. Each spun his horse around with lightning speed for a second pass. Thundering again, the stallions reeled up and charged in unison. Colliding, Kamura with katana drawn cut Saigo's spear in two with one swift cut. Both samurai turned their mounts once again, poised on the grassy bank, stopped, and dismounted. Their steeds backed away as if they knew the battle was now only for their masters to decide.

They stepped forward with both drawn swords, the daito (long sword) and the wakizashi (short sword) held in each hand. They worked their way toward each other in deep powerful stances, holding firm their honorable resolve to use their steel life-taking blades held high above their heads to crush the enemy.

Foot movement resembled that of snow cranes as the men moved within mortal striking distance. Closer they came as the intensity soared between life and death until their sword tips touched, circling and moving cautiously through the river grass and gravel, bodies primed, muscles strained. Then in a flash General Kamura lunged while his spirit yell echoed through the valley and above the sound of the river. Kiai! The sun reflected off the swords to the samurai watching from above. The two generals clashed and collided in a single moment, then Saigo shifted to the side, ducked down, glanced his sword off Kamura's sword, and with expert mastery horizontally cut the midsection of his doh (breastplate).

Kamura fell and rolled to the left. Rising on one foot and one knee, he once again held only his long katana high in the air. Stallions stood motionless behind them awaiting the fate of either samurai. Saigo sliced his katana through the air, cutting Kamura's sword in half, then instantly drawing his sword once again overhead, cut downward in a vertical cut to sever the shoulder. Kamura darted to the side, landing on his ribs as Saigo missed the mark with his katana and landed hard atop Kamura's body. Neither samurai moved for the moment. Then Kamura pushed Saigo off and stood up next to Saigo's flank. Saigo had landed on the end of Kamura's broken sword, which pierced his belly.

Kamura reached down and, grabbing Saigo's breastplate, pulled him close as Saigo's weakening eyes fixed on his. "This is karma," Kamura spoke softly. "The sun grows strongest at the last instant, my Saigo."

Saigo replied, "Please finish me, the men are watching."

General Kamura stood up, observed the thousands of samurai holding their position and watching above, moved his gaze to the reflecting stream, and drew his short dirk from his belt. He said, "Yes, Saigo, it is my karma," as he thrust his blade into Saigo's neck. Then taking his short sword, wakizashi, he spun it around several times in the air, then stopped and sliced Saigo's head off and held it high for all to bear witness to.

Holding the head in one hand by its hair, he replaced his wakizashi, then picked up his daito (long blade), turned, and walked to the stream. Holding the head of Saigo out to his side and his sword in the opposite hand, he strutted to the stream where he washed the head off in the icy water. There he mounted his stallion, and carrying the bodiless head, he rode up and down the river with his trophy shouting, "Kamura, conqueror of all Nippon." Turning, he rode up the mountain to his warriors and elegantly positioned his horse at the opposing samurai and stood silent as they began to retreat to the mountains behind them. One life for 20,000.

My reverie was interrupted. "Now Jack-*san*, remove your *uwagi* [uniform top]. It is time to start." I could feel the extreme pressure mounting in my mind and *saika tanden* (stomach) as my *ki* began to increase. My heart raced as I positioned my body in a solid stance for *sanchin* breathing that Sensei explained to me. With his guidance, I positioned my feet as told and began to follow precise instructions, using deep forceful breathing combined with powerful exhalation. There I was to stand solid in mind and body against all the elements of nature. I raised my arms from a low position in front and then reaching with my arms extended, clenched fists high above my head, I exhaled in full force in one slow, pragmatic, isometric movement, pulling my arms downward and across in a sweeping and cutting motion in unison with exhalation. Every muscle held itself tight as if to be unconquerable in its rigidity to any pain and against the odds.

I continued. Sensei instructed me to inhale deeply as I brought my arms high above my head on each count. "Fill your lower stomach first, Jack-*san,* then let your lungs expand to the maximum," he said. Hands above my head, lungs filled, I would pause momentarily, then exhale forcibly on the next count, drawing my arms down in time with my lungs, diaphragm, and every muscle possible contracting to become what Sensei called "steadfast like a mountain." As I followed Sensei's directions, the air was suppressed within and rationed out as it passed from my lungs, though my throat, and out in an audible way that sounded strange but powerful.

Before I exhaled, Sensei first showed me the proper way by demonstrating this dynamic aspect of the *Budo* way of *kokyu-ho.* As he thrust his belly out and filled his powerful lungs, he tightened and exhaled as though a typhoon flashed through the room. I noticed sparrows and starlings fly from the windowpane and trees outside in momentary fear as Sensei bellowed out the archaic, high-pitched wind of *sanchin kata-kokyu.* It was amazing and hypnotizing at first. With each breath, he became inconceivably more invincible and compelled to connect mind, body, and spirit in the universal way. I was totally moved in every aspect by what was taking place.

After about three or four breathing rotations, I found myself growing stronger. Beads of sweat began to pour from my skin. It wasn't long before I was instructed to change my manner of exhalation and force to different levels as a storm on a sea rises and falls with the rhythm of nature. I seemed to be moving into a new state of mind, where I was present but not present. Feeling myself drift into a world of unknown depths, I did exactly as my teacher instructed me to do, never allowing myself to doubt his guidance or question my security. Minutes passed, then half an hour, then I lost track of time. I now calmly focused a softer wave of breathing as I learned this new way, and then was told to hold my breath for a brief moment. Sensei said, "Relax, Jack-*san,* and take one instant to just float, to remain fixed in position."

"*Hai,* Sensei," I said.

He then instructed me, "This time, Jack-*san,* I want you to attack the enemy with all your heart and never give up. Both *katanas* drawn, lances at your side, you are to be as if a thousand warriors in battle with an invincible, unyielding, super-spirit. Do you understand— *wakarimasuka?*"

I responded, "*Hai,* Sensei, *wakarimasu.*"

Now he was shouting out his commands and I responded and focused my *sanchin* deep within my heart and tightened every cell of my body to shape the blending of nature and the call to the *bushido* code. Veins popped out of my skin, then the tendons and ligaments in my neck strained to the limit, screaming for mercy while the thunder of the soul met time and moment. Blood rushed through my arteries and to my head as I turned deep crimson red, while my upper chest followed in kind.

The deep hissing growl that echoed through Sensei's *uchi* bounced off the walls and down the hall. I visualized the neighbors stopping in their tracks as if an eclipse took place then turning toward Sensei's house with disgruntled looks, saying, "Well, he's at it again."

I slipped into an entranced state of mind, seeking more from within my grasp, when to my astonishment the distant thunder became ominous. Halfway through my exhalation phase, two boards crashed upon my shoulders, then two more in time with Sensei's roaring *kiai.* My body shook as if an earthquake hit, and once again I was rocked, this time with short, five-foot two-by-two's across my back. I heard the clear crack of the wood as it shattered, the pieces flew as splinters and chips across the room, but no pain.

Sensei thundered, "Hold your spirit strong and brace up, Jack-*san*. Give me more *ki!*" Next count, I drew in my breath sharply and seemed to feel more powerful than I had ever known, and for a moment could see Sensei stepping in front of me with large cinderblocks. Holding one at a time, with several behind him on the floor, he now prepared to disintegrate each one against points on my concrete frame. Holding my arms high in the air as if to burst with my breath held tight, his count rang out and his *bushido* command came forth where I tightened once again under the pressure and exhaled *(haki dasu)* with all my might. My stomach strained with victory and my heart filled with the indomitable spirit of the *Budo* way. With my arms drawn halfway down, a cinderblock exploded against my forearm, then another against my thigh.

My arms became extended when three slats of pine, one stacked atop the other, were gathered together and held as one. Sensei jumped high in the air then down came the boards crashing upon my forehead. My entire body shook again and again, this time driving me a foot or two backward toward the wall, but I froze in place.

"*Motto kiai, motto kiai,* Jack-*san!*" Sensei yelled. He was asking for more spirit—in simple terms, more gut—to connect with the powers of concentration and the source of the cosmos.

Then I was instructed to use punching-*sanchin*. This was where I would slowly punch using the isometric and dynamic tension coupled with my *sanchin kokyu* (breathing methods).

I felt a magnificent peacefulness come over me, yet still I maintained my immovable low-slung stance. The burning sensation in various areas over my body seemed to tingle and come alive. I inhaled on command and drifted into the magical state of *mushin* (no-mind). The freedom of existence seemed to overwhelm me. It was as if I drifted out of my physical body and rose above myself to see the action taking place. I watched as I pulled my punch back to my hip on command, then again the blasting count to exhale and tighten rang out. At last came the power of the ancients, out poured the heart and soul of my love for the *Budo* of truth. Then the smashing of two-by-twos, one after another across my forearms. Each time my fist was extended to the limit my arm would reach, the wood exploded in all directions. The arm shook, the fists turned white, and an uncontrollable sensation filled my essence. It appeared in slow motion, the arm glittering with sweat, vibrating wildly, then the two-by-two slicing the air from high up, coming down, smashing my forearm, and behold, matchsticks flying in all directions.

From somewhere, a roundhouse kick struck my body across my solar plexus but I stood the blow. Another punch was followed by several more riveting my ribs, but I withstood the pressure. Counts rang out, sweat ran from my face, and my lungs felt as though they would rupture, but I stood my ground.

Sensei hollered, "*Yosh!*" (Good!) and then shouted, "You have died, Jack-*san,* and returned. Now maybe you're reborn, *hai!* Relax and breathe, *shin kokyu—shin kokyu.* Now we must research your journey in *sanchin kokyu no gaku.*" (The study of the *sanchin* breathing way.) I stood motionless but very clear, then collapsed in a heap on my knees. There on the floor in the home of my teacher I waited to return to my normal state, if there still was one to be found.

The *samurai* leaned on their swords covered with the blood of their battles. Victory or defeat was all they knew. To live by the sword, to be loyal in serving, and to die. The sweet taste of victory and the triumphant state of the heart had been won. How glorious the attainment of the highest ordeal in life—to find the human heart. Truly the "Highest Pitch of Vigilance."

I thought of the true warrior spirit. I wondered and thanked God above for the gift of life which served as a means to find myself. I remembered the Japanese monastery and the Buddhist monks of Mount Hiei who are known for their austerity as the marathon monks. My ordeal had been similar.

Each day in a ritual that lasts 1,000 days over a seven-year period, these Buddhist mountain monks rise early in the morning at 1:30 AM and run from eighteen to twenty-five miles through the night. On and on they charge, regardless of wind, snow, or heat, over part of a mountain which is known to have the most treacherous slopes, an area of the mountain known as the "Slope of Instant Sobriety." Because of its intense and penetrating cold, it instills a great mindset, making the mind as though it were a piece of the mountain itself.

The traditional color of Japanese monks' robes is black, but these mountain monks wore white, the color of death. This color is worn because of the great possibility of death on the slopes at any time. This thought is continually with them, permeating their existence. The obligation to never fail is recognized as one of their ritualistic goals, so they carry with them a sheath knife, or as the *samurai* did, a small dirk and a portion of line or rope. This is a constant reminder that if they fail, if they don't meet the task before them, they are destined to hang or disembowel themselves. The fear and dishonor if they did not succeed hung over them.

I thought of how my journey to accomplish the same end was taken over and over again in the *dojo* and in the martial arts way. It was always a means to purify the soul, to forge the awakening of the spirit, and cleanse the mind.

Clarity of life and the reality of love are found in the moment of truth. The monks on their journey find themselves at the end of the 1,000-day crusade with the final task of a nine-day fast without food, water, or sleep. Through this ultimate austerity, they perceive the value of human existence and return to life with the brilliant understanding of one's purpose. These journeys were all seen by me as a means to awaken the innermost sanctuaries of the human soul. Each time, I became more than fascinated by my quest and its end. I attempted and succeeded to look at my quest in life as the path to achieve the fleeting moments of happiness.

I looked up at Sensei and said, "The long and extreme road to enlightenment never changes for the *bujin*, does it, Sensei?"

He replied, "Jack-*san*, each road leads to another and another as you have seen. Now you can start your new journey. Go change up and we will go to lunch for Japanese *tabemono*." I spent perhaps an hour cleaning up the broken and shattered materials all over Sensei's home and taking the remains out to the alley, finding tons more materials out back. Never a moment without practice in my teacher's life, and I was becoming like him. How proud I was on that day.

Returning to the house, I cleaned myself of wood chips, cinderblock bits, and other objects that had lodged in my skin and stuck to my back. I observed the welts, bruises, and minor cuts covering my body. I felt as though the battling *samurai* I had wished to become was now closer to the indisputable warrior mind, the monks of Mount Hiei, or the *samurai* general on the plain battling for his honor and more. I reached for a new crescendo in my life and drove forward with the enlightened passion of a new absolute foundation shaped in my heart.

Some of the other materials used in testing my nerves and the strength of my mental discipline would be saved for another time. Many of the bruises and minor pain began to set in as I picked my uniform and equipment off the floor. Battle wounds and scars in martial arts are not always seen during the engagement, but become most apparent after you have traversed the mountain. Sensei noticed my upcoming trauma and mentioned, "Jack-*san,* you will no doubt be sore tonight and perhaps tomorrow, but your mind will be elevated to a new level and the bare essentials of human endurance. Take these Chinese herbs and use them whereever you have pain and it should eliminate the problem overnight."

I replied, "*Arigato,* Sensei." Taking the bottle, I observed the contents and Chinese *kanji* on the label, then slipped it into my pocket.

Sensei then took me into his den, sat me down, and explained in interesting detail the meaning behind *sanchin.* As usual, I began to take notes about the historical value and moral meaning of everything that I experienced. Over the next few hours I would enjoy *o-cha* (tea) and *sake* in an attempt to relax and soothe my advancing aches. I knew one thing for sure—martial artists are crazy. I have never doubted this truth for one moment. Off to the restaurant we went.

Sonkei—Respect

CHAPTER EIGHT

First Words, Then Blood: The Battle of the Total Darkness

Chi wa mizu yori mo koshi. Blood is thicker than water, so the saying goes. This is the story of an unforgettable night in my early days of training. After acquiring my black belt rank in *karate-do* a week earlier, Sensei had informed me that there would be a special free-sparring session held at his *dojo* for *kotekitai* (body-toughening). I had just begun to heal from injuries sustained during the recent siege of advancement to my new black belt rank, and as usual, my teacher abstained little from his battle-ready consciousness on this occasion.

I arrived at the Detroit *dojo* late in the evening. Things were uneasy in the inner city, so I drove my old clunker and parked it close to the *dojo* front door. At night the streets were bare, except for the occasional streetlight that wasn't destroyed. An automobile lay jacked up on blocks from a swift stripping, now without doors, wheels, or bumpers. It occurred to me that it may have been a Mercedes at one distant time. I was sure without looking that the seats and sound system lay in someone else's hands somewhere in Detroit.

I stepped out of my car, looked around ominously, and locked the doors. I smiled for a moment then chuckled, "Why lock it?" With my duffle bag and gear inside, I trekked across the street to the *dojo*. I could hear the freeway growl in the distance where I just got off about an eighth of a mile down the road. Another car sped by me filled with crazies, fortunately not stopping to offer me any assistance. The *dojo* was dark and silent. No neon sign signaled me to approach and check on classes, only the ever-present vertical steel bars and black planks of plywood used as security, all of which ran from the building's corners to the top of the once-formed windows. Constructed of solid brick, the building appeared more like a fortress than anything else.

Down the block I could see several young teens headed in my direction from the corner liquor store. Reaching for the door, I found it locked and was thankful Sensei gave me my own key. Any time a student becomes a black belt and trustworthy, a key is offered so he or she may practice on off-class days. This allows admission to the training hall and a chance to engage in more personal practice without the interruption of other classmates or Sensei's piercing gaze.

In the olden days, one either trained in group classes held at specific times, or trained at home. Private time in the *dojo* allowed privileged students the opportunity to groom *kata* and strengthen weak links in the battle chain to gain proficiency. Class was never solely enough. If one were to survive, specific steps were necessary to master the martial art and cultivate the personal responsibility to charge ahead full-steam.

The group of teens came closer and started yelling at me about something. Ignoring them, I reached deep in my pocket and found the single key. Quickly inserting it into the lock, I turned it, but nothing happened. Did I have the wrong key or had it jammed? My heart began to race and it seemed I might be in for some unexpected combat. I turned the key again as they stepped on the curb twenty or thirty feet from me, The door opened and I passed through. Strange as it may seem, silence fell outside as they passed by, even though the door swung open behind me. It was later that I learned that no punks ever attempted to enter the sacred ground of the *dojo* lest they find themselves most certainly in harm's way. The lights in the locker room were on, but the *dojo* was still dark. I removed my shoes and placed them in the proper receptacle for footwear found in most traditional *dojo*.

I felt an awareness of icons past and sensed the eyes of *samurai* standing at attention with their chins tucked and *chonmage* (topknots) secured in place. The old building with its twelve-foot ceilings loomed overhead. The traditional office to my left was quiet and without light passing through the *shoji* screens. I shouted, "Sensei, *gomen nasai?*" (Are you here?)

Then the deep answer came forth. "*Hai,* Jack-*san*, in back, in the battle room with Toyama-*san*."

I smiled, "*Daijobu,* O.K., I'll come back."

I stepped onto the *tatami,* being watchful as I walked only near the very perimeter. Etiquette did not allow an individual to cross the mats in civilian clothes. It was upon these same *tatami* that I would learn the meaning of rebirth *(taishi ichiban)* and face death from time to time. These mats also bore the silent cadence of the *kata,* the forms in practice found in all systems of Oriental martial arts. Simply stated, *kata* has a deep and meaningful history behind it.

The Japanese have been conditioning their behavior and attitudes more than a millennia. It is in this process that beliefs have become so deeply rooted. The philosophical and spiritual side of this behavioral conditioning was based on the combination of Shinto, Buddhist, and Confucian precepts. The physical side of the programming was based on the precise set of "cultural molds" called *kata. Kata* means "form" and is the mechanical process of doing things. The precise way of doing things became ingrained in the societal evolution of the Japanese and thereby became the meticulous fashion of performing any act with demeanor.

Kata as I know it became one of the pragmatic guides in the quest for ultimate personal development and the means to understanding oneself. *Kata* became the essence of specific rituals and conditioning in and out of the *dojo.* Examples of other *kata* include the ceremony of *chado* or "the way of tea" (the tea ceremony) and *shodo,* "the way of calligraphy." For martial arts, it is important to understand that all styles of Japanese and Okinawan martial systems were comprised of specific *kata,* all sustaining themselves with their inherent etiquette and conditioning. It is said that when one performs any task or duty, it is done with exact fashion or *kata*. In the *dojo* we forced our way into formidable mindsets by doing these ancient forms, and everything soon became *kata* itself.

Walking to the back of the *taijo* I stepped over various wooden two-by-twos, all about seven feet long. I wondered at the use they would play this interesting night and what evening construction Sensei had planned. I entered the locker room, passed through it, and while doing so smashed into a chair in the dark which caused me to drop to the floor, holding my foot. I held my pain in, then stood up. I heard Sensei say, "Watch out for the chair in the middle of the floor Jack-*san*." I replied, "Too late," and a slight chuckle rang out.

Entering the private chambers of my teacher in the rear of the *dojo,* I respectfully knocked and said, "*Gomen kudasai,* Sensei." (Excuse me.) He said, "Come in and sit for a moment with me and Toyama-*san*," who was a stout student in his thirties, stocky and bald. I had fought this opponent on the *tatami* numerous times. I had seemed to draw powerful and decisive spirit from within during our furious conflicts on the *taijo*. Toyama-*san* had been in Sensei's *dojo* some time before me and had trained for many years. His duty and performance in things of a *Budo* nature was honorable and forthright.

I decided from the beginning to outshine him or anyone in this manner and attempted to win my teacher's full attention and respect in every way. I wanted to become the *shosei* (star pupil) of my *sensei*. In Japan, this would be likened to becoming the *uchi-deshi,* or live-in pupil. It was to be my destiny. In this quest I sought out the *Yamato Damashii* or already possessed it.

Yamato Damashii is the Japanese fighting spirit as it is known in *Budo,* or, more commonly, the spirit of Japan. *Yamato* is the original name for Japan, and is written with the same ideograms used in the word *wa* or harmony. It could also be said that *Yamato Damashii* translates as "Spirit of Harmony." This hard-line practice forestalls weakness and fortifies the meaning of a strong will to win and survive. I wanted to be all of that. Becoming the *samurai* possessed by these traits forced me into being possibly the most aggressive practitioner in the *dojo*.

I was learning to become victorious at heart and accept the way of most resistance as the means to learn in the original manner. This takes simply guts, the one key to success in any endeavor, and must be based on an inexhaustible spirit to win. It is important to understand that the most difficult task is usually the best to formulate an unstoppable heart and mind. We most often find that the general attitude when the going gets too rough or demanding is to turn away and give up.

Never give up or allow your mind to slip. Failure to demonstrate an extraordinary spirit in pursuit of a goal, be it sanctioned or otherwise, is regarded as shameful in the Japanese society. Learning the *kata* of the *karate-do* was difficult but not as arduous as mastering the *kata* of the *Nihon*-way (Japanese way).

I sat on the floor atop an old *tatami* in Sensei's quarters. Toyama-*san* sat across from me. The room was small but had the flavor of old Japan. To my right was a worn-out rice cooker slowly steaming some rice *(gohan)* that Sensei had recently prepared for a late-night snack. Sensei offered me a cold Asahi beer which I accepted. I was told he had some interesting practice set for the night. I couldn't even begin to imagine what was in store. This was the first time I had come to the *dojo* with the intention of any battle late at night. Toyama-*san* had the appearance of one of our old ancestors in the *karate-do* lineage, so he was called Toyama-*san* from this likeness. His real name was Dave. His eyes were deep-set and offered the semblance of an Oriental appearance and style. Heavy-set in the midsection, he had good power but unworthy stamina because he carried too much weight.

Actually, he seemed to be what was called in Japanese *bushisuke na yaru* (rude fellow). Both of us carried a similar grudge that Sensei wouldn't tolerate in or out of the *dojo,* and he informed us that tonight both our attitudes would be dealt with. Questions filled my mind. As we sat, Toyama-*san* went through a few large beers and began to get huffy about his battles in the streets and carried on as though he were a master of endless duels. I heartily laughed and just stared at what was to become my opponent later that night. His arrogance began to work on my nerves and Sensei mentioned, "Toyama-*san,* no more *biru* [beer], you now need to prepare for some intense awakening. Go wash your face."

Toyama-*san* responded, "*Hai,* Sensei, I will."

In the ancient art of *kenjitsu,* it was common that the duel to the death was a man's way to honor. It was called *shiken-shobu* (duel to the death with live blades). Sensei spoke of this often, as the old ways were always interesting and mysterious. It was equally amazing where Sensei himself came up with all the archaic practice methods. Never a dull moment in personal abuse. It is said that the old masters were known to be somewhat crazy from the actions they led in life within *Budo* and *bujitsu.* I found out as time passed that I too would take on the wild spirit and become one of those few known as *kichigai* (crazy). I loved the practice of *kotekitai,* so tonight became just what I expected — a night in heated discord which I would always remember.

Sensei said, "You know, men, practice only in the *dojo* or under familiar circumstances can sometimes be counterproductive, so tonight you will practice or, I should say, go to war, in your street clothes in and out of the *dojo.*"

"What do you mean, 'out of the *dojo,*' Sensei?" I asked.

Sensei responded, "In *karate-do* we have a tendency to become too accustomed to the atmosphere of the *taijo* or in general the *dojo* itself. Therefore, it is important to face our battle in uncontrolled situations as well as new and different environments."

He continued, "In real battle, one is not going to slip into his *keikogi* or stretch out in preparation. One must be in a state of readiness at all times. There is an old Latin phrase which states, 'He who desires peace, prepares for war.' So tonight will be a test of endurance."

I remembered a quote from my recent reading.

> It is a doctrine of war not to assume the enemy will not come, but rather to rely on one's readiness to meet him; not to presume that he will not attack, but rather to make one's self invincible.
>
> —Sun Tzu, *The Art of War* (c. 500 BC)

Over years of training and becoming more seasoned to the way of battle and the way of life, I've learned that the ready state of mind requires the strongest positive, constructive approach to conflict. By facing in the most diligent manner that which is most demanding, without any cant or whitewash, we improve our state of mind and gain the most ready state. In life one must accept all challenges and circumvent the trap of self-pity and unreasonable fear. One must never look for readiness in the future, but must be ready in spirit and attitude in the present. It has always been difficult to take a concept of philosophy and make it work. It is too easy to allow tomorrow's promises of hope to deter one from the intense requirements of today's moment.

All I knew was that it wasn't practice that makes perfect, it was perfect practice that you focused your energy on and hoped perfection would be born.

Tonight I knew I had to determine the disposition of my opponent and ascertain the correct field of battle engagement with all my soul. I must prevail to win against the arrogance and pretentious air of an individual who needed a lesson in manners. I assumed Sensei had planned this for a long time because of the hostilities that were building over months of practice. Even I had to be knocked down a notch or two. There was an old Japanese saying that goes something like this, "If the nail sticks too high above the board, then it must pounded back down." Perhaps this was one of the times I was to be pounded!

"Now go into the *taijo* and start to warm up," said Sensei. "I want 2,000 *makiwara* first, then 1,000 *maewashi-gerri* on the *makiwara* next. By the way, no lights during *makiwara*." I thought he was kidding, but soon found out he was serious when he angrily came out on the *tatami* and flicked the switch off. Slowly growing accustomed to the darkness, each of us began a vigilant striking program with either foot or fist. At first, I could barely see the striking post, then over what seemed to be several minutes I was punching full force without any mishap and only occasionally losing my focus and concentration. I began to realize the importance of this training regime as I hammered away. One becomes desensitized to all that is going on around him but still remains aware of his surroundings. I was actually developing *mushin,* no-mind. *Mushin,* as it was taught to me, is the cultivation of the clear mind, or the mind of one who retains no thought at all, but still holds a clear and exact perception of one's connection to the universe.

As I executed each separate blow against the straw sheath, the echoes of two boards smashing against each other riveted the *dojo.* Echoing from wall to wall, it was the systematic ritual of *dozen* (active meditation). The *makiwara* used in our system was made of two clear oak planks about five feet tall. The two boards were placed upright in a steel base bolted directly to the concrete floor. Separating the boards was a smaller two-by-four about a foot high which allowed the hardened oak monsters to slam together as one struck the front oak plank. It was covered with hemp or old *obi* (*karate* belts) to add somewhat of a cushion for the contact. In the beginning, your hands seemed to disintegrate under the impact and your knuckles became bloody and bruised. The *obi* were now blackened with the crimson blood from years of battering and testified to the conflict students waged during individual warfare day in and day out.

As I hammered away, I drifted from a clear mind to the wisdom I have found over the years with hands of iron and knuckles of concrete. I found myself on an endless journey to places unknown, yet fully aware that I must keep on moving to find my original nature.

The mountain rising up from the valley in front of me raced toward the heavens with forceful breezes singing through the pine forests. I stood determined to conquer the highest peaks, to wind myself through the jagged rock and seek the higher learning of the self. Halfway up the jagged slope I stared behind me at the distant raging rivers I crossed earlier, now appearing calm and serene, carving their ways through green pastures and towering pines.

Peace and tranquility spread over the valley as though nature felt love and wept for all those who attempted to win but would not find the way.

A bluish haze filled the air from peak to mountain peak, so thick you could almost reach out and gather a handful of its essence and feel its wonder. I felt the battle winning, I could sense the highest summit still not knowing exactly where it lay. Each muscle ripped with pain and agony, but still I forced myself onward with the heart of a Spartan Legionnaire to conquer the unknown peak. I would achieve my victory. With gendo-ryoku (the driving force), I sought to endure, and my will to perform pushed me beyond human endurance at all costs.

On reality's plane, perspiration fell from my body as I tore into the core of the *makiwara's* soul. By now my eyes were accustomed to the slightest detail in the *dojo.* I could see the most indiscernible item such as the mouse who sat in the corner next to the *tatami* watching with frustration in his eyes, no doubt confused, unaccustomed to the banging of the *makiwara* so late in the night. I now swung into full force and switched to the roundhouse kick, making little change in my breathing and not hesitating or breaking the pace. Onward I drove myself. I noticed Toyama-san now faltering in his movement, most likely from a lack of conditioning and the repercussions of the beers he put down earlier. I soon began to struggle as well from the cadence and remembered the *samurai* parable *"katte kabuto-no-o o shimeyo"*—fasten your war helmet tightly even after a victory. This saying warns you to be aware even when success is yours.

I reached my bloody hand over the rim of the rock, touching more firm rock in my struggle to the summit of the mountain, and sighed. How much further?

Then in the back I heard: *"Matte, matte."* Sensei commanded us to take a break. Close to an hour must have passed and midnight was approaching. With lights back on, it seemed the sun had broken through the clouds in a blinding flash. I remember how I had to prepare my eyes with night-vision goggles in Viet Nam before going on lookout duty or night security watch. More than seeing whatever you looked for, you had to sense things. Now in the art of *karate-do* I found that this became more important if I was to win in battle. My existence was in an arena of warfare.

Sensei said, "Grab the full-contact headgear [*bogu*] and gloves only." This ancient headgear appeared to be the counterpart of the actual *kabuto* (helmet) used by the *samurai* of old.

Sensei said, "Both of you are to don your *men* [headgear], arm pads, and elbow gear as well, then full-contact *kote* [gloves]. What you will be practicing is full contact, primarily battle to the head areas. Be sure to fasten your *himo* [ropes] tightly around your heads because you will be doing this while in the dark." We stopped and stared at Sensei. "That's right, no light—full contact—in the dark, just as though you were engaged in the alley. So fortunately you will not have to go outside behind the *dojo* tonight for this specific practice." *Some relief,* I thought.

My sweatshirt was soaking wet and my oversized exercise pants were equally unmanageable. I seated myself in the traditional position on the *tatami* and began to secure the armor in place, making sure no *himo* came unfastened. When first placing the armor on your head, the *himo* made you feel as though you were choking, but over time you came to understand that a tight helmet saved a broken neck. If this fight happened in the dark, I would most likely get my head ripped off by any powerful blow as the gear became sloppy on my shoulders. Quitting meant I would lose face and may have to succumb to extra-intense discipline, all of which I was not in the mood to subject myself to. I now pushed myself to what would be "The Highest Pitch of Vigilance." I wanted to be the one with the legacy of "he who never gives up."

"Knowledge without action is not knowledge at all," as the *samurai* maxim goes. One must engage in the most critical conflict to understand the indisputable truth of the real self. *Conquer your fears,* I told myself. The lights still hung on as Sensei prepared us for our night battle. I looked through the small steel bars placed across and woven into the faceguard of the *men,* which served as a barrier between me and the explosive charges of techniques that smashed with contact to the head area. With the headgear twisted and turned in a few places from thundering past blows, I wondered at my fate.

I now faced a ledge in the mountain and had to conquer the challenge. I repeated in my mind the words "gendo-ryoku, gendo-ryoku, gendo-ryoku." Focusing on the sound of my breathing, I rallied at the ordeal of holding fast the thought of ultimate success.

I reached up for a tree limb that hung from the ledge above as my hands, now worn and tired, began to sweat with the possibility of losing my life in the fall to emptiness. One thrust of my body against a rock and I would be on more level ground, a better means of meeting the challenges ahead. I turned to see an eagle whisk by my head, as if to say, Climb, climb, the ultimate limit awaits you.

I picked up my padded full-contact gloves, slipped one over my fist, and began to lace it up. As I placed the other one on, Sensei approached me and assisted with the lacing. Toyama-*san* was finishing his preparation for battle when Sensei shouted, "Time for battle, *ikimassho!*" He positioned us a lengthy distance apart, approximately fifteen feet, then approached the center between us and gave us some simple rules. "Everything goes, no one stops unless I say so, and you do not give up. Do you understand, *wakarimasuka?*"

We both blurted out, "*Hai*, Sensei, yes, *wakarimasu.*" I attempted to visualize everything before the lights went out, but I knew it wouldn't help. Nerves began to sharpen, the mind became intensely sharp, and all my senses began to coil like a spring being compressed. As we both bowed to each other, I knew I would be blinded as the lights went out and have to sense things for brief moments before I became accustomed to the dark.

Off they went. Toyama-*san* rang out a *kiai* and rushed forward in full force, letting go a blitz of techniques hoping to hit home. I dropped low to the ground and at the last moment sidestepped, wheeling a hooking kick through the air, but I missed him as he flew by. I squinted my eyes to see, but then realized I must allow my senses to relax and feel my way clear to the target. When you don't see the blow coming, the most damage is done. I slid down the wall making a sound to attract my opponent. I felt if I drew him in, I would be able to use my tactics to deceive his mind. Once again, a charge and I exchanged with him. We collided in mutual contact, holding on to grapple against the wall. Our headgear made contact, and I launched a series of elbow smashes to the head area, feeling two maybe three find home. A fist connected with my midsection near my solar plexus. Bang! I felt it once again. I reached up and wrapped my free arm around his headgear and then twisted my hip to throw him. As I forced him to the *tatami,* resistance was increased. Another fist made connection with my back as I grappled and held tightly for the throw.

Then slipping my leg around his, I found leverage and brought him down. Into the *tatami* his face went under his headgear. Dropping like rocks, we both drove ourselves into the mat when we heard Sensei shout, *"Matte!* I still do not hear anyone screaming for victory," he said. "Move to the center and start again." Winded and weary, we found an area to stand our ground and start again. Hitting the *tatami,* I felt a warm stream of fluid seem to cascade down my face inside the headgear. "I am surely sweating heavily," I told myself.

My mind reeled instantly and I struggled to gain vision and power. The storm ensued once again as Sensei shouted, *"Hajime!"* It was as though his voice came from high above me in the distance. Where was he during all of this?

Both warriors moved with caution and emptiness to unleash an attack. Leaning to the right, then to the left, I maneuvered into any position redeemable in the light of triumph. My self-will and thirst to find my target heightened with each moment. My eyes now seemed adjusted to the darkness. I could see shadows and sense heavy breathing, or in another moment hear the feet in a rush against the *tatami* mats. I was learning to distinguish action with senses other than sight alone.

Instead of being in a traditional *dojo,* I felt as though I were in a chamber, enthralled in a one-to-one battle for survival. Again my head seemed to break my concentration and spin for an instant, but I moved forward. Then I heard a mad rush to my rear, but it was too late—Toyama-*san* was upon me striking with all his force, using knees, elbows, fists, or anything in which he could propel me to the *tatami.* Turning was indeed difficult with the weighted headgear restraining me from spinning around to forestall the wave of the attack. I spun around leading, with my elbows, and connected to the side of his helmet.

Two more elbows came crashing against my head, then another partially blocked to the chest. I covered then, grabbing Toyama-*san's* inside thigh and his sleeve, then body-slammed him into the wall and down into a pile of equipment stacked up in the corner from the last *dojo* class.

At that moment, I found a greater spirit within me which seemed to advance my thinking to become victorious against any odds. I had to maintain some degree of momentum. The mountain's summit was now within sight. The winds began to whip at my face and cut into my ribs. The harsh cry of eagles echoed from canyons below as they climbed high into the skies above, beckoning me upward, still upward, at any risk to find my glory. Balance was of precise importance in the last few moments. An ideal vision came into my head as I forced myself not to look down at any misfortune lest failure overtake me. Long-range perspectives of this ordeal gave way to the momentary expectation of success. My thrust in the climb became a domination now of the self, and my opponent was only a stumbling block, a rock in the way to an end. No narrow perspective, only a clear view of my intentions remained in my pursuit. In balance, I repeated the words hisho—hisho—hisho (decisive victory), and now made a clean path to victory.

The balance of battle turned. I launched knee thrusts one after another, then grabbed Toyama-*san's* wrist, slammed both legs across his body while he was on his back, and stretched his arm across my inside leg as I laid back against the *tatami* and pulled with all my force for a joint controlling technique. Stretching across the *tatami* entangled in a web of conflict, I saw that the ledge of the summit was in my grasp. I pulled myself up, and his scream of *"Matte, matte!"* filled the air with his torment. I rolled over to see the sky clear and blue as I reached my hand for the heavens and touched the face of God.

Sensei shouted, *"Matte!"* The lights flew on, almost blinding both of us. I had wrenched Toyama-*san's* shoulder and we both lay there in exhaustion for the moment, not knowing who exactly or where we were. "Jack-*san*," said Sensei, "Stand and go to the center. Toyama-*san*, you do the same." Half-crawling, or I could say half-dead, we made our way to the center, bowed on command, and were instructed to remove our *men*. A piece of the steel faceguard seemed to rip my face as I removed it, only to find blood the crimson color of battle streaming down my face. Apparently the steel wire somehow dislodged itself and penetrated my head during a forceful blow.

Sensei grabbed a wet towel and motioned me to remove the rest of my contact gear and come to his private quarters where he would clean my wound. Slowly, pragmatically, I lay my battle gear on the *tatami* in a neat pile, as martial arts form in detail remains ultimately important. This was etiquette. Stoicism equally shared a place hidden within the contact gear and one's heart. Remain stoically reserved *(enryo)*.

My mission to find a part of my true self had become a reality. Toyama-*san* was now heading for the men's room to leave his late dinner in the toilet. I hoped that he realized beer and verbal battle can sometimes create a false illusion of certain victory. Nothing in life is certain.

Later that night, around midnight, we told our stories and asked questions—a reward for battle-stricken Spartans. I finished with a cold one, and listened in quiet awe to the historical education Sensei passed on to us.

The raging fires had subsided, the torrential storms had become calm, and my unruly spirit found passage to a wiser state of being. The climb down the mountain would be filled with a sense of honorable satisfaction. I prepared for my journey back home, wounded but with a song in my heart. One story among a hundred was to be remembered and told over and over again in the presence of those young warriors who some day would meet the most formidable opponents and find victory or defeat. I pressed onward and thanked Sensei for the punishment and enlightenment found in the recent journey, and began the trek home.

Jin—Benevolence

CHAPTER NINE

Real Kung Fu, Please

The small city of Drayton Plains lies in the center of the lower peninsula of Michigan, where my *dojo* was located. Not a completely rough town, but it has the usual Midwestern mentality, and most of us grew up with rowdy football players and so-called greasers. I belonged to a small car club fraternity in high school, so I knew most of the people who lived in the county. Everyone was going into the military at the time of my graduation and there was no reason why I could not come to my country's call and perform my duty as well.

Everyone wanted to go to Viet Nam and play hero, and I was one of them. No one really knew what they were getting into, and the odds of returning from the war were not in your favor. I was fortunate and perhaps Buddha was watching over me, so I brought all my experience and knowledge back with me. The real risk I found could never be satisfied by sitting, hiding, or watching from the sidelines. My personal history opened the door for new martial arts discovery and adventures at the hand of the new *sensei,* the *samurai* of *samurai,* I would soon meet.

Upon separation from the military, I sought out the best *dojo* I could find. After a long search I finally discovered my present system of *karate-do* and *Budo.* Training in my early days was intensified to a twenty-four-hour ordeal. You were on what was termed "on call." This meant you were ready for practice at any time during the day or night if your teacher called. The hard-line *sensei* I discovered and the one who took me under his wing made the decision to teach and guide me personally as his protégé. I was honored and practiced daily in the hope of continuing my life task of finding my true nature.

Sensei Brian Frost, by whom I was honorably accepted, is a true *Budoka* in his own right. My encounters with his unbeatable spirit I will soon relate.

After the years of basic training passed and my expertise increased, I opened my first full-time *dojo* and began a fresh journey in the land of my birth. This *dojo* was formidable, designed for battle-oriented students, and it housed the strongest and most willing practitioners I could find. In this Spartan *dojo,* the walls were reinforced for contact. The cement walls were painted and served as a shock barrier when our bodies slammed against them in *kumite.* Traditional *makiwara* lined the back of the *dojo,* where the neighborhood stood witness to the cadence of fists smashing the boards day in and day out.

Contact equipment hung from the wall ready to be used for total cultivation of striking skills and mastery of kicking. Everywhere you could find an object specially designed to increase your battle-ready condition.

One particular week, I had been working the heavy bag diligently to increase my striking stamina and movement. It becomes commonplace to recognize the bag as only a target, but you must come to understand specific things in general. A heavy bag does not strike you back. A heavy bag is not going to take your legs out or cut your face. A heavy bag does not have the capacity to rip your groin open with a front kick. It only takes it while you dish it out. The alternative is difficult to undertake, but in simple terms, you must fight opponents to truly know.

You must learn to subjugate yourself in full-contact battle before enlightenment appears. Defeat must be experienced so that rebirth can take hold. In Japanese, this is called *taishi ichiban* (to be reborn, or rebirth).

"This [*taishi ichiban*] is an old Zen saying which is known in aikido in regard to the evasion of the opponent's attack. One is to regard the mind as nothing and without thought or to abandon the mind and renounce the actual self. This deals with the death of the self in self-abandonment, or the killing of the delusion which has afflicted the mind."

Only when you find yourself exhausted and close to failure will you find the real self, the unstoppable spirit. Self-realization happens under intense pressures with a mind that is receptive and open to changes. As you become accustomed to the rigors of *Budo* and adapt to the persevering way, an awareness or open-mindedness begins to fill your being and shape your character in the most positive way.

That day on the heavy bag was brutal, and it was on that same Friday night that a telephone call came in. I answered and spoke to a man named Guy Chen who told me he was professionally trained in *kung fu*. I challenged his mind for a moment, digging for information, and asked what type of system he practiced. He mentioned that he trained in the original *kung fu* Crane style, had training in *Shotokan, isshin-ryu, kempo,* and *shito-ryu,* and was looking for a place to practice free-sparring. Even today, you still find the honorless and rootless less fortunate practitioners who do not even realize they are the laughingstock of martial arts. Back in the early 1960s, it seemed everyone knew *kung fu* or had some previous instruction. I usually designated this as "T.V.-*fu,*" and considered the sources. Only in America could this happen. It seemed everyone became Chinese masters for a period and responded with a claim to fame. The charlatans were everywhere attempting to cash in on the martial way, the esoteric mysticism, and many still make that claim to fame today. Now of course, it's a more sophisticated breed, one which mixes the politics of conservatism or liberalism as a platform for their theories and ideas.

Using deception and misrepresentation, all those who believe themselves to be demagogues or magical supreme sages use their bought and twisted knowledge as a means to usurp the uneducated. "They fell victim to their own cancer then and still do now."

The true warriors of old still stand as monuments to the historical values and traditions passed on to them. They remain in the quiet reaches of small communities, passing on time-honored culture in the pursuit of real virtues.

Recognition for unique skill in *Budo* or some specific fighting martial art expertise truly never achieved was genuinely common in a society that based its strength on the way you could talk that talk and walk that walk. Judge me by my actions, not by my jaw, I was once told.

I invited Mr. Chen down for what I hoped would be a lesson in the so-called real *kung fu* and hung up. Doubting that he would show up, as many do not, I taped my hands from blistering and had one of my shins wrapped from excessive conditioning. So it seems—every time I find a unique challenge, I start off in a battle-weary state. It must be some test of my moral will and courage. Those who design their lives after battle-ridden *samurai,* as full-time martial artists, live in a contact state of unceasing injury and healing. You'll also find some who injure themselves in practice going for lengthy layoffs, which hinders their growth and enlightenment process. Great difficulty is found when attempting to play catch-up.

In actuality, one can find ways to train areas neglected as a result of damage in other areas. This perseverance gives rise to the Japanese term *tegiwa* (skillful). If a *kenjitsuka* (one who practices the way of the sword) executes a winning cut in the most highly purist form, it would be mentioned that he was *tegiwa.*

I returned to the *taijo* to continue my workout with the two students who were waiting for me. Two of my small group of superb technicians were referred to as "Rock-and-Roll." I hammered these boys as much as possible in the hopes of witnessing their graduation some day to black belt level. With both of them at attention stance, I spoke of certain qualities they were cultivating. Philosophy was a broken record and to varying degrees uncertain for me in those early days. I was learning and practicing the way *(do)* of my life in the great hope of conquering all my fears. My two brown belts were soaking wet as was I from our free-sparring. Bloody uniforms covered our bodies and bruises were erupting on our chests and arms.

This ritual of self-abuse came with each dawn and ended late at night. Every moment was a learning experience in the game of survival focused on *karate-do.* I spoke to the boys, "Gentlemen, in our quest for knowledge, one must be willing to face adversity and conquer a weak mind. The demanding and perilous path seeking the universal warrior spirit means facing the worst of adversities and skillfully moving forward. We must never lose sight of our goals as *budoka,* which are to shape our character, face the storms of adversity, and cultivate a peaceful mind."

Just then the *dojo* door opened and who but the real *kung fu* "master" stepped in. I motioned for the boys to hit the showers and see me on their way out. We exchanged bows formally, and separated from our task. I stood alone with the new arrival.

Walking into the *genkan,* I approached this master teacher of *kung fu.* Standing in front of me was a five-foot-ten stocky guy in his twenties. He sported a small scar on his cheek, and I noticed soft hands, no doubt from a lack of forceful training. He most likely employed *kata* practice only as a means to gain every martial strength. It may sound strange, but one day I actually had an individual walk through my *dojo* door seeking information dressed like a *kung fu* warrior, only he carried a bamboo flute. I almost lost it for the moment. Any time the door of the *dojo* opens, it presents new surprises that keep me amused. I was not surprised to notice that this visitor wore the traditional Chinese *kung fu* attire, with slip-on *kung fu* shoes, buttons and all. I sarcastically introduced myself as he did and asked if he brought his uniform to change into. "This is my uniform and should serve as the means for me to gain new knowledge," he said.

I chuckled inside and answered, "O.K. Come into the training hall and loosen up for a bit while I take care of business. A couple of my students are going to leave and I have a few words to share with them."

Back in the locker room I told my warriors to stay and watch if they wished. Honorably, both requested to remain in the *dojo* and get a new glimpse of their *sensei* in action. They had felt the wrath of my fist and foot many a time and now wanted to watch another fall victim to the full force of my martial arts mastery, no matter the level of proficiency. I motioned for them to go to the *genkan* and lock the door, not allowing any stranger or student to enter. Puzzled, they looked at me momentarily and bowed, saying, "*Hai, Sensei.*"

I was gifted with the ability to grasp things easily from the very beginning of my *karate-do* journey by observing closely. I understood later the benefits of this in developing the art of *meitorigeiko* (observation practice). Insight to things connected to *heiho* (tactics) is important, as it allows the universal concept of *Dairokkan,* or the sixth sense to be tuned through cultivation of my art. Often in Nippon as well as with my *sensei,* the senior or head instructor of a martial arts class would appear momentarily to demonstrate a *waza* (technique) of special significance. If you were unable to grasp its meaning, let alone the technical movement, you lost invaluable knowledge and time. In order to keep from losing anything relevant, one practiced this art with intense focus so the slightest detail was ideally retained. It is common for a *sensei* to show the *waza* briefly and usually only once.

If one were chosen to demonstrate the *waza* afterward and made a foolish mistake, he was normally ejected from the class in a dishonorable way for the night or week. Intensity was based on aspirations which filled the practicing student with strong will and emotional ties to both *dojo* and *sensei.* These ties or acts of bonding are called *kizuna. Dairokkan* was the award gained by years of determination and fortitude.

I took a few minutes to wrap my left hand, which had been injured during practice. I found my mind spinning with various thoughts of strategy and decided to put this would-be *kung fu* madness to an end. My monkey-mind started to take a position of clarity and my breathing intensified for battle. Into the *taijo* I entered. This was my ground, my turf, and my battle area. I was ready for my personal history to unfold. I moved smoothly across the *tatami* and casually began a methodical stretch repeated thousands of times before. Moving left to right, I observed from the corner of my eyes his deep stances and strange sparring guards against which I would match my talent. I never questioned my martial art or the faith others had in my skills.

Snap kicks and punches were his vital forte, so it seemed. I, on the other hand, displayed my ability in falls and rolls, and just to warm up, I found my way to the *makiwara* where I launched 200 or 300 punches to get my adrenaline flowing and pumped. I motioned

Mr. Chen to move to the center of the *taijo* and ready himself for *kumite*. Mr. Chen asked, "Do you wish to *kumite* full contact or light contact?"

I paused, then said, "In the course of my study, I have found that contact disallows any foolish doubt hidden in darkness of the mind to be smothered and dispelled."

"Please contact; I feel my control is very good, as I hope yours is!" said Mr. Chen. He added with some more condescension and arrogance, "Tonight I will apply what has been called superior fighting strength known as the 'drunken monkey.'" I smiled and thought, *Dead monkey, you mean.* My two students now sat on the side of the *tatami* holding their stomachs.

Mr. Chen then fastened his black sash securely, which I had hoped to wrap around his neck momentarily to choke him with. I grunted *yoi* (ready). He said, "Let's go!" I began to circle when he shifted from a guard position to a low stretching posture as if to mock me in my foolish attempt to strike at him. Side to side he moved, just as he said, in a monkey-type form. I thought that the best thing about this may be that he won't have far to fall when I deck him. I executed a few low kicks to draw him out, when he jumped up and snapped some jabs at my head. As he punched, he made this hissing noise. I figured it was used to distract the opponent or throw off his tactics. In fact, it was ridiculous.

Once again, he punched at me jumping up from the *tatami* when I launched a roundhouse kick to his bicep and connected. Solid it was, and he dropped his arm, switched sides, and fell back into his deep stance. So much for the use of his arm.

Up again he came this time partly on the ground and partly in the air, spinning around and around, executing hooking back kicks and sweeping to catch my legs. Again, I figured this tactic was supposed to make me dizzy, but I sidestepped and moved to the wall, where I darted to the left as his body slammed against it. Bouncing back, he found himself in a drunken monkey daze. Both of us found our way to the center once again. I noticed his wind growing heavy when he struck at my shin with a side kick from a low position. I jumped up instead of back and stomped his foot into the *tatami*. His brief yell was followed by, "One moment please." I was growing tired of this.

I roared, "Let's get the lead out—move it!" Next I launched a full attack—jab, jab, jab, jab hook. Then he countered my front kick, I blocked, and countered to his solar plexus. *Kiai!* My spirit yell discharged. *Ippon* (point), and I felt my fist sink in his midsection. Down he went gasping for oxygen. I stood at the side of the mats waiting for him to gather his thoughts. I did not attack at that point, resolved to make this a fair battle. Red with anger, Mr. Chen blurted out, "I thought you said you would use control."

I responded, "Mr. Chen, that was control for us. Now quit your complaining and continue." Next we centered and circled. Once again he came at me filled with rage and deep-heated anger. I blocked a few kicks and then allowed him to strike my midsection as well, but to his frustration he was unable to drop me, move me, or create any victory.

He stopped and said, "Point."

I asked, "What point are you talking about? I'm still standing."

"Once again then." We both moved to the center of the *tatami*. I had the best results in my *kumite* when I fought next to a wall and that is where our fighting headed. Moving in a series of jabs and Chinese kicks, he attacked once more in a frustrating attempt to put me where he wanted, down. I was growing tired of picking at my opponent now and planned an attack for a choke or sweep. I had just begun to move in when he once again jumped into the air and launched a flying side kick, *yoko tobi gerri*.

In a quick subtle motion, I diverted my weight and ducked under his jumping kick. Grabbing his sash, I pulled him full power to the ground as though he had a wire attached to his waist like a stunt man blown back from an explosion. Down he came smashing into the wall and tumbling to the concrete floor outside the *tatami* area.

Clinching tightly, I pulled and spun him around on the floor as though he were a top, then stopped and launched two powerful reverse punches back to back in the rib area. He collapsed in a mass and lay there attempting to gather his senses and breath. I was more concerned with the wall behind me that now had two gaping holes in the dry-wall where all the stud work showed and plastering hung. I immediately felt the frustration of having to repatch my battle-weary *dojo* again. It was only last week that one of my senior students blew a direct hit into the same area with a kick that missed his partner.

I focused my mind back on my opponent, who still lay there in a heap, perhaps regretting the long hours spent assimilating what he had believed to be a noncompromising fighting system. He stared obsessively at the mats, confused. I motioned for my two students to come to his rescue and help him to his feet. Quickly my seniors rushed to respond. As they rolled him over and assisted him back to his senses, I noticed blood flowing from the cheek where he made contact with the floor from my *nage* (throw) and a bulge in his rib cage, no doubt from the punches I unloaded. Perhaps a few broken, to say the least. His sash of Taiwanese rayon was ripped in pieces and lying on the floor beside his feet. I made some comment like, "Do you want to go a few more times before I go to dinner?" He glared at the floor while my boys helped him to the lobby. I then said, "Perhaps not."

I remembered how I had once been confused and frustrated from a battle I fought long ago and how the knowledge I retained then was believed to be the most splendid. I found myself half dead, in a pile on the pavement from an attack I initiated in some jealous rage. Two broken ribs, a fractured wrist, a torn shoulder muscle, and I would require numerous stitches for my facial injuries. I somehow recovered and vowed to seek out the master technician to show me the way. Fortunately, I was lucky enough to consummate that journey. I was driven by honor and swore to become indomitable.

In my journey I gathered the intrinsic energy to conquer my spirit *(seishin)*. *Taishi ichiban* (rebirth) had been my salvation. I was thankful to have found my guide, the *samurai* of *samurai,* as the solution to my immediate frustrations.

I faced Mr. Chen in the *genkan* and said, "You can never set conditions, limits, or controls in a battle-ready state. The only thing one must do is win with honor. Our greatest achievement is to strive to know ourselves, to master the ultimate challenge of the mind and crush petty grievances and egos that limit our existence. No one lost tonight, Mr. Chen. In fact, you may have gained the most in your last hour of this life. My object was to find my weakness of spirit and my flaws in battle. I can now move on with new insight to find my way. Please come back again if you wish. I would hope you and I may learn more aside from humility and honor."

I opened the doorway and bid Mr. Chen farewell. I sat down in my office with my seniors, who questioned my strategy, hoping to find new resolve in their practice. Over the evening we sat in my office, shared *sake,* talked of full contact, and spoke of *bureiko* (old war stories), as I had learned to do from my Sensei.

That night we cleaned up the damage temporarily. One wall was destroyed and had to be repaired, three photos in the lobby fell from the shock of bodies smashing opposite the lobby wall, and one mirror was cracked. I began to think the entire *taijo* should be padded for future battles.

> Boldness governed by superior intellect is the mark of a hero. This kind of boldness does not consist in defying the natural order of things and in crudely offending the laws of probability; it is rather a matter of energetically supporting that higher form of analysis by which genius arrives at the decision: rapid, only partly conscious weighing of the possibilities. Boldness can lend wings to intellect and insight; the stronger the wings then, the greater the heights, the wider the view, and the better the results; though a greater prize, of course, involves greater risks.
>
> —Major General Karl von Clausewitz, *On War,* 1832

Dojo—Compassion

CHAPTER TEN

West Side Blow-Out

Friday night had been a long night of practice and I found my way home quickly. The *dojo* was packed the night before and I had pushed an advanced class hard on conditioning in order to present the next phase of *kumite* using endurance practice as a teaser warm-up. After class, everyone paired off and began what is called *jyu-kumite*. In this type of practice, everyone in the *dojo* finds a partner and on command begins the hard-line training of contact with little attention paid to control.

Everyone was already fired up and in many cases burnt out from the intense hour of class warm-up using basics *(kihon)*. Once class was completed, all were forced to commence straight-on, heavy-duty battle. The *taijo* area appeared to be a monastery training area straight out of a James Bond novel. Spartan warriors clashed from wall to wall. *Kiai*s roared from one opponent to another in universal conflict, placing deadly blows focused to vulnerable points on their human targets. Bodies flew against the walls and off the mirrors.

After three minutes passed, everyone exchanged partners and repeated the encounter. I backed off the mats and let the would-be *samurai* exchange volleys in the hope of winning their match. I watched the high-level spirit of juniors and the way the advanced practitioners dealt with the pain of contact and continued in the hopes of mastering mind and body. Uniforms were always drenched in sweat, while some students bloody from a wild mishap continued on in their search for ultimate domination. The beginners sat along the sidelines and stood in mirrored areas to serve as a moving buffer should the fighters fly in that direction. Action was seen and heard at every turn with the heightened acute awareness of full battle. I loved every moment of the action. The boys had strong hearts and a great willingness to win and cultivate their expertise.

The more advanced students were now engaged in heavy, heated battle. I watched, stopping and starting two senior *dans* (black belts) who grappled to the back wall, when in an instant a spinning kick launched by one of them blasted another hole in the drywall.

I stopped them momentarily to mention that construction detail would take place as always early Saturday morning. They knew what I meant, stared at the gaping hole, and then continued more carefully. The training was hard, but even more difficult was the ability to concentrate fully on the subject, time after time, until external considerations faded from the mind. I showed a variety of new techniques to many students, but realized it would be futile to continue until they learned to use what they had already been taught.

I had strived to build a training hall of awareness and perception, one that embodied the ritualized, concise practice of everything connected to the way of *Budo*. It was important to maintain a seriousness of combative intuition and an acute sense of honor in all one's actions. In the midst of battle, everyone struggled to develop *zanshin*, or the profound and perceptive state of mind before, during, and after attacking or defending. In a deeper sense, this was the "remaining spirit." Everyone sought this emotion, as it allowed the mind to respond more freely in the midst of continual action. As you became more focused on your tasks without your mind being cluttered, you also became more responsive to the activity occurring around you.

"This crucial sharpness allowed one to follow his or her true course in life by releasing the clouded mind from frustration and finding clarity."

I looked across the *tatami*, viewing with pride the numerous heated battles, and I was reminded of the special purpose of a true *dojo*. The blood, sweat, and willingness to climb the mountain at all costs, to gain the ultimate level of personal achievement, became the glue holding us all together. It was the common denominator within each living soul in the *dojo*. We all pushed to master the sharpness yet also the peaceful ability to govern our own individual belief in the self, a master plan to give us honor and freedom to think. The *sensei* was the benevolent dictator, carrying the torch while pushing the force to the highest level of combative skill.

The training room itself exemplified simple beauty. Okinawan weapons were held on a rack on one side of the *taijo*. The picture of the Founder was on the main wall keeping watch over our efforts from a venerable station high above. The full-contact fighting armor *(bogu)* was lined up on another wall. Blood-stained, bent, and twisted, it loomed over the action waiting to be subjected to indisputable punishment. Floors covered with traditional *tatami,* worn and tattered in places, taped in other areas, presented a sense of realness, that of the Eastern way.

The effect of the *Budo*-style atmosphere was one of a reverberant remote hall which overwhelmed by the absence of significant decoration. This was a place devoted to serious one- and two-man war. Everything was positioned exactly to represent, in the most classical sense and manner, the true roots of those who showed the Way before. Unlike the glossy sheen that modern-day assembly-line *dojo*s represent, a master of *Budo* offers the reality of a connection to all things.

"Those who reigned in total devotion to a worthy cause knew their legacy would go on to be remembered throughout history, unlike those who chastised or slandered the original way, the way of loyalty to his mentor."

This was what I struggled to bring about and vowed to never lose sight of. Very specific goals were to be met one small step at a time. This way, the foundation of true virtue could be found while traveling on the right journey. I aimed to promote the open mind by use of the empty hand.

In the office the telephone rang. On the other end was a kickboxer acquaintance who had severed his ties with traditional martial arts and decided to seek his fame and glory in the ring. I had little regard for this avenue of martial arts. It was a life of little spiritual development in *Budo*. Rather, it meant a life bent on the destruction of an opponent with fame and fortune as the goal. Kickboxing had its combative nature, which a traditionalist loves, but lacked the human compassion found in guiding others in the universal way. Foremost, it was an uphill battle for years, followed by a fall straight downward in the end. At any rate, each must seek his own level of conquest in life, and so I accepted that. I chose to focus on the art I was involved in. My art was one of details in strategy used in brutal practice.

The caller told me that there was a major nightclub called La Notte's in the town of Sterling Heights that used the competitive ring as a draw for its customers. The caller invited me to arrange a martial arts demonstration as entertainment during intermission. I usually shunned these opportunities because they were just that—entertainment. Usually, those watching had little regard or understanding for the years of skill it took to properly execute the traditional techniques. Also, a bar audience never seemed truly appreciative of anything after maximum alcohol consumption. In any case, I owed the caller a favor and could possibly draw a member or two for my *dojo*. Most of all, it gave my students a chance to engage in one of the mysterious aspects of the *Budo* Way, and this offered new possibilities for them all to look forward to.

Before the novelty eventually wore off in the early 1980s, kickboxing was at an all-time high and its practice was found in every major city and sports network nationwide. I thought perhaps I could introduce something unique that would turn a head or two, as showmanship wasn't really my forte. Saturday night was generally the big blast in metropolitan Detroit, and three advanced students and I all prepared for the demonstration. I decided upon the infamous bed of nails. Done many times around the world in other *dojo*s and at exhibitions, it offered a sense of excitement and realism as well as a window into the esoteric side of martial arts.

The board had been custom-built. It was comprised of approximately 740 razor spikes. The maze of spikes had been painstakingly riveted into place, set less than an inch apart on a thick plywood base.

The board was approximately eighteen inches wide by three and a half feet long backed by pine on the reverse side for support. Each wooden side had been glued together so the spikes were securely seated and sealed. This prevented any spike from slipping sideways and possibly ripping open anyone who placed their back upon it. Lying prone on the bed of nails, one's back becomes the pin cushion and penetration point of entry if the individual flexes in fear or moves in the wrong direction under pressure. Weight had to be distributed to the entire back area, and relaxed calmness was a principle of *ki* necessary to allocate even distribution of weight stress.

The demonstration consisted of me taking the reclined position on the bed at the fight's intermission. Thereupon, I would have approximately 100 pounds or more of concrete slabs positioned across my chest, solar plexus, and stomach area in two or three distinct groups. These slabs in turn would be reduced to cinder ash as my advanced students attempted to destroy each stack with a loaded sledge hammer. Luckily, I had done this time and time again for one reason or another without any major fear in my preparation. The main concern for me was always the hammer man. Would he deliver the maximum power and thrusts for a clean break? Would he hit me, the target, square?

One distant memory I tried to discourage had a tendency to return to my mind. A certain brown belt whom I had required to practice the striking format weeks before another demonstration smashed concrete on my chest and somehow slipped on the lowest block, grazing and almost smashing my groin. He was replaced by another student as my assistant.

On the appointed night, my students and I arrived at the club and entered the parking lot behind the bar. We saw others rushing in for the spirit, excitement, and the visual experience of full-contact martial arts. Entering the club, we were greeted by my friend and made our way to the back rooms where boxers, managers, and trainers gathered in preparation for ringside battle. There in the crowded room, we all began the ritualistic game of preparation. My mind drifted. My first bed of nails experience had been a fearful encounter....

Sensei Frost called me to his back quarters while I was practicing *kata* late one winter night. He said, "Jack-*san,* please lift that thick moving blanket on the floor over there and bring it to me." "*Hai,* Sensei," I said. I reached down, picked up the blanket for Sensei, and to my astonishment the amazing and infamous bed of nails loomed into view. I caught my breath because it was the first time I had been permitted to view it. Most beds of nails were large enough to cover your entire back when used, but this one was small and compact, which meant the force of any blow would be concentrated into a smaller area. More danger and intensity, I quickly came to understand. I reached down and placed my palm hand on the nails and found them unexpectedly piercing. Removing my hand, I looked to see several indentations along the base of my palm heel.

"What do you think, Jack-*san?*"

"It looks scary, Sensei, and not something I would want to do," I told him.

"You're right on both points, Jack-*san.* Just so you don't think it's some kind of joke, you can lie down and try it."

I said, "No thanks, Sensei, *domo,* you're joking, so I'll wait for a day in the distant future when I'm more prepared."

Sensei said, "The distant future comes all too quickly for many of us, and yours has just arrived. Tonight you will see the major reality of the *karate-do* bed, Jack-*san.*"

Sensei told me to remove my *keikogi* top and go through *sanchin kokyu* (forceful breathing). I couldn't believe I was doing this. I now began the most compelling type of esoteric breathing I knew and learned long before I made my first level of black belt. Sensei cautioned me to tighten with each exhalation and squeeze my diaphragm and stomach muscles with all my force. "Harder!" he shouted. *"Harder!"* I did several compelling exhalations many times on his command, and then twenty or thirty punches flew into my midsection. I thought I'd explode on the impact of his fists, but penetration was minimal, no doubt due to his control, and I survived. After what seemed like a dream, Sensei threw me a major curve.

"Okay, Jack-*san,* now lie on the nails slowly as I guide you down."

Shaky and somewhat fearful, I lowered myself on the steel rack and, descending, I felt the first row of nails begin to pierce my back. Sensei shouted "*Osu!* Lie down now."

"*Hai,* Sensei," I answered. I found my mind and body immersing into a single action and then in a position never before encountered. I had made it, I had overcome another fear. Then slowly Frost Sensei stood on my stomach and chest and carefully walked around, shifting his feet. He pranced lightly, reciting some gibberish that I couldn't understand. Sensei then counted, "*Ichi, ni, san, chi, go, roku, shichi, hachi,*" and so on. This went on briefly. Then he jumped off and said, "Let your mind clear. Let your thoughts disappear. Go back to where you have no memory, no conscience, and no feeling. Disappear, Jack-*san*." Then finally he said, "No big deal, Jack-*san*. Let's have some Sapporo."

I rose and was overwhelmed with excitement but tried not to show it, though I must have been beaming. I crossed over a new frontier, a vast ocean of personal self-belief where few are allowed to stray. I found a new reality in the blinding wind as the desert turned to total darkness, became deadly still, then allowed light to be born.

So it was, in the dark hours of the night, my *sensei* had carefully guided me each step of the way through the "bed of nails" ritual. Things always seem difficult the first time, and so it was with me. I survived the ordeal with many minor puncture wounds, but few that dampened my quest to challenge other adversity in my journey for ultimate *karate-do*. The bed of nails built for me later on was one of danger and a challenge which always ensured enlightenment. I had seen some on which the nails were filed down, dull, and in some cases even cut off. It should be mentioned that this demonstration, like so many others, was only used as a medium to test the concentration, mind control, and the concrete resistance to unfavorable danger and pain. It expressed the explosive power of martial arts and the precise skill in executing dangerous feats of mastery. It was no true equal to the combative quality and expert ability of the *Budoka* one met in combat. Individual warfare was in itself pure enlightenment by actual means.

On this night at a bar in Detroit, a few of the fighters were gathered in a corner discussing the events of the evening and slipping on fancy silk pajamas used for kickboxing. Still others wore stars and stripes, a disgusting example of martial exploitation, and placed rubber contact gear on their feet and hands for protection.

I began to change into my traditional uniform, worn for years and never altered except for the tattered sleeves and soiled and slightly ripped lapel from continuous grappling or throws in the solitude of Sensei Frost's *dojo* or my own. Slipping on my *zubon* (pants), I noticed Kenny, a familiar kickboxer I had met some time ago. This was his champion match, his stepping-stone to the ultimate level of competitive achievement. I didn't see eye-to-eye with him, and his air of cockiness was expressed as he looked my way. He asked me if I was going to fight, knowing very well I wasn't, as if to challenge my authority and expertise. I responded, "No, I'm here for the simple purpose of giving the spectators an undoubtable taste of realism." He sneered at me and began his ritual warm-up.

Now Kenny wasn't any great monster, but he was quite fast, aggressive, and determined. The problem was that he did not fight enough in bare-knuckle contact during his junior years. This type of training solidifies one's belief in the self and in the way. This training is the blueprint from which an individual can seek the highest form of personal growth and understanding through intensive practice in the old-fashioned way. Kenny weighed about 165 pounds, and was about five-foot-nine and very ripped. His practice was extreme, but again his ability to penetrate and the maximum resistance his body could withstand would not do for the best of the best. This was common in kickboxing circles where technicians never mastered true warfare and found themselves seeking the glory of fame in the ring as an alternative to *Budo.* Take a look at how many kickboxers own a *dojo* nowadays long after their quest. Kickboxing is a means to an end. It's just not the end I was searching for. At any rate, the challenge is there for those who wish to be a part of the game and its celebration.

A devious idea crossed my mind. Perhaps I could take part in a very valuable lesson.

I recognized that Kenny did not embrace the type of austerity valued by my mentor. He apparently had no time for the learning of inner discovery which enhances the value of life itself. If one can go where few others dare to go and overcome ego-related distractions through hard physical training, one can discover the world within.

"It is through a firm mental resolve following a combative related path in which one must forge a true grasp of fighting traditions. Seeking to find the ultimate truth in the form of conflict and chaos can only be understood when one immerses the self deeply within one's own mind of study. The only way out is in, and the way to enlightenment is mastering our understanding of the egoless self. The continual domination of facing fear and pain during body-toughening allows a reality to appear in the midst of uncertainty only if the danger in training is great enough to expose the light. This is the vision of awakening."

I shouted moderately across the room. "Hey Kenny, would you mind warming me up a bit with some of your kicks and punches before I get started? It helps me gain some momentum, you know."

"Sure, why not," he answered. While he was not yet prepared in full dress for his battle, he had on his foot protectors and had taped his hands. His trainer asked him to put his gloves on, but he declined saying, "First I'll warm this guy up." I knew he didn't train in the form of fist hardening and the possibility existed for injury to occur if he made improper contact with my body. I immediately knew why his trainer was disgruntled about the lack of gloves.

Pulling my hands up and standing with my back to the wall as if I were in my *dojo* or in a ring, I pulled my arms up high to expose my midsection and asked Ken to throw in a few punches and kicks. I focused my breathing and started to exhale in short breaths known as *kumi-kokyu* or "fighting breathing." I coordinated this with the rhythm of his attacks. This allows one to use forceful exhalation *(haki-dasu)* as a means of anticipation to battle contact while in the center of the actual conflict. It also helps clear one's mind and in some cases psyches out the opponent.

I calmly and nonchalantly directed my gaze at Kenny and said,

"Please Kenny, more power and don't let up. You needn't concern yourself about my welfare." Techniques came flying in as bare knuckles and all made contact. I could see he was becoming concerned. "O.K., Kenny," I said, "Stop joking around and give me all you have." Again Kenny launched his attack. Full-power punches drove into my midsection, and I stood like an oak tree.

"You know, it's time for you to do your best and I don't appreciate this special consideration. Now full power, what's wrong with you? I need to be pumped up, Kenny!"

He began to turn red with rage as frustration set in. I could see his confidence and hostility start welling up inside and his composure was starting to show signs of disintegration. He was defeating himself without knowing it. I now had him exactly where I wanted. His trainer shouted for him to stop. He kept pouring it on. Everyone in the room now stood motionless watching.

He backed off for a moment catching his breath. "You know, if that's the best you can do I believe you may have a major problem tonight," I shouted. "Now give me your best shot!" He became enraged and started to blow out.

Just one more technique, big Kenny, I said to myself, *just one.* It was then that he loaded up and threw a knee kick in. I tightened and dropped the end of my elbow down close to my ribs for cover and locked it into place. Slam! His knee collided with my elbow, jamming my forearm against my body, and it was then he was in trouble. He showed some extreme pain, but attempted to hide it. I said, "Thanks, Kenny, that's just what I needed."

His trainer pulled him back and off to the corner of the room. I accomplished the strategy I had planned from the beginning. His record was 30 and 0 when he came into this nightclub, and before the night was finished it would become 30 and 1. He lost in the first round by a knockout. What happened to him after that I can't say. But once again, the reality of true *Budo* made it clear that one must never lose sight of the true way.

The nightclub was going wild from all the excitement. Intermission had come and that meant I was up next. One of the nightclub hostesses came into the warm-up room and announced, "Jack, you have a couple of minutes until show time." Then the moment came and my students and I headed to the club ring. Everyone was screaming, drinking, and carrying on as if we weren't even there. No doubt the liquor was having its effect. We climbed up the steps, through the ropes, and onto the canvas. We began to lay out the demonstration format. The lights burned brightly, and slowly the sounds and presence of the audience in the bar began to disappear in front of me as my task became more defined. I sat in the formal seated position and began to meditate above the roar and laughter going on around the ring.

One of my students brought forward the infamous rack of nails, allowing those close by to touch and inspect the nails. I remembered how "the Price of Integrity was always determined by Eternal Vigilance," then the crowd became quiet and I rose to explain the demonstration. The lights silently flooded my vision again as the staging area became the arena for my exhibition.

Now standing in the *sanchin* stance, one of the oldest forms of *karate-do,* I began to reveal its true nature as others looked on. Breathing in *sui-komo* and exhaling *haki-dasu* loudly and sharply, the air entered and forcibly left my lungs. My stomach heaved, then my shoulders as I exhaled aggressively in preparation. Two of my students picked up five-foot two-by-twos, stood to my sides, and drew them high behind their heads. My mind cleared and gave way to the mysterious no-mind *(mushin)* as though victory had been seen and achieved during a battle-ridden moment. It was then that I was jerked back into the present. Reality hit home.

In an explosive moment I stood as a granite wall while two-by-twos slammed across my midsection, throwing pieces into the air and out of the ring into the crowd. Again, I stepped forward in a circular fashion. Then I executed a dynamic tension punch slowly, forcefully, with muscle working against muscle, shaking and shuddering until my extending punch locked out with all my force. I tightened and exhaled with all my inner strength of *ki.* Then instantly, another two-by-two came crashing down across my forearm, breaking into pieces while my arm extended motionless without a flinch. Another board slammed into my forearm from above, shattering around me. My *ki* now was in full force as my mind became as clear as a summer morning wind. The mountain was now ready to be scaled as the main event began to unfold. Silence fell across the crowd. Perhaps I had stopped their brains for a single moment.

I looked into the distance again, unaware of those present and then aware as my mind slipped back and forth into the existence of my mission. The crowd was nowhere to be found nor did the sound of laughter, shouting, or heckling enter my mind, if any existed. I was alive and alone with the universe. I turned my back to the spectators and moved toward the infamous bed of steel. Kneeling in front of the board, I made my destiny clear. I would traverse the fissure. My mind was completely free of thought. I was here but I was nowhere. *Kojoshin o mote* (endeavor to excel) darted across my mind. Then I stood, turned my back to the rack, sat down and stretched out on the bed of nails without hesitation. I glistened with sweat and lay motionless as my assistants quickly began to stack concrete slabs across my chest. One upon another was positioned until five or six rose high above me. Slabs approximately eighteen inches long by eight inches wide and two inches thick were readied for the crushing blow to be delivered. Another stack began to build across my midsection at this point. As the weight increased, my breathing became shorter and more defined. The pressure was mounting. Students kneeled on each side supporting the stacks in place.

My trusty hammer man stood tall, lifting the heavy sledge above his head, momentarily holding it there, then he shouted out his *kiai*. Through the smoke-filled air, the sledge cut downward and slammed into the heart of the first stack. Cinders and concrete flew in all directions. My *kiai* blended with his as rubble fell to my sides. Then, in another instant, the second smash of steel rained down against concrete making the smashing connection, and, as before, cinders flew in all directions. I became alive and felt as strong as an anvil yet as yielding as water. Resisting and giving, blending and changing as the will of nature, I completed my journey.

The crowd stood quiet and motionless for a moment, then my assistants reached down, grabbed my arms, and pulled me up as bits and pieces fell from my chest. Standing, I felt victorious and relieved it was over. Then, applause hit me in the face, forcing some reassurance of my task and victory. A less doubtful crowd now stood before me. The extremely leery and intense character of the crowd gave way to smiles and acceptance.

We all bowed and left the ring for the changing room. I picked up a towel, wet it down, and wiped the chips and fragments from my body. Kenny was there, a champion who met his fate. He said, "Where's your *dojo?* I'd like to come out." I understood his thirst, but realized he would never see the inside of my *dojo.* Sometimes the strongest are the last to change.

I turned to my boys and said, "*Domo arigato,* gentlemen. You did us all good. I'm very proud of you. Let's go have a beer at the Japanese restaurant and speak of *Budo.* Perhaps we can meet Frost Sensei too." It was a good day to be alive.

Yuki—Courage

CHAPTER ELEVEN

The Thousand Pounds Victory

Training in the traditional way, one must acknowledge the existence of life—of strife and conflict in human affairs. The rationale of *karate-do* is to acquire the ability to transcend the fears of aggression, pain or injury, and death through the mastery of a self-defense discipline. This practice enables the *sha* to defend oneself in rational form and do less harm to others; hence the ultimate fighter and martial arts master is able to skillfully control violent confrontations through the precision of technique. This is the essence of devoted practice and of mastering the way. As one learns to see and react, to clearly define responses in violent intentions by others, both in a physical form or through verbal exchange, he is able to evade and redirect the force of the enemy or opponent.

"Whoever said the task would be a walk in the park?"

Tesshu Yamaoka, one of the greatest swordmasters at the turn of the century and in modern-day *Budo*, focused on the ultimate centering of the mind and its universal power. In the development of this process he instituted what was called the *Seigan Geiko* or vow practice. *Seigan Geiko* forced the practitioner to focus on the ritual of total development based on intrinsic oaths. This loyal goal-seeking theory led to sincere and vital determination to succeed.

A glimpse back in *samurai* Yamaoka Tesshu's time captures this severe training and austerity in its timely purpose. The first type of *seigan* was a period in which the student practitioner had to complete a 1,000-day training routine in austerity, followed by contests or *shiai* which involved the continuous engagement of 200 opponents. When and if this *seigan* was completed, the student warrior was allowed to face and endure a 600-match *seigan* over a three-day period of austerity. This was not the end. If successful, he would attempt the highest-level, a seven-day, 1,400-match battle.

This historic extreme of *Budo* practice is a severe attempt to find the ultimate realization to the inner self and the training fit to capture the inner spirit. After reading this, you should endeavor to ask yourself, "How difficult is my practice to find *satori?*" Each must pursue a means to achieve the highest level of mental control by seeking *satori* in his or her own life. Continual vigilance must be born of mind and body, never allowing failure in the vow one has taken. Find your most difficult physical task in past training, multiply by 1,000, and an idea manifests into your reality. This is *Seigan Geiko.*

The snow was coming down full force as I turned onto the street to the ascetic warrior's home in Detroit. I knew that Frost Sensei had something special planned because it was late in a day on which the *dojo* was not open for practice, and the last words he mentioned were "time for *Rentai Ho,* or acquiring a sound body."

I pulled up to his home, stepped out of the car, and encountered the melting slush that stuck to my shoes and soaked them thoroughly. I was always one of those guys who wore tennis shoes in the winter, no jacket, and sunglasses to look cool. In actuality, I froze and wasn't too wise about watching my health from time to time. Alas, youth often makes us feel immortal. I knocked on Sensei's door for over an hour and sat on his doorstep between bouts of frustration and chill. Sensei finally came to the door.

I wondered whether he had been taking his afternoon nap and asked him where he had been. A disgruntled answer came, "I was testing your patience, Jack-*san*." He continued, "You may have to wait all night for a secret now and then." I knew what he meant. The test of nerves, will, and attitude was augmented by more than mere practice of the physical body. One was taught to conquer the mind and to make it right, so that right action both mentally and physically was the payoff. I instinctively learned to accept Sensei as he was, with and without the flaws which showed through. Passing judgment on his character and slipping from my journey were never allowed to enter my spirit. Greatness was found in subtle ways and means. Few patiently shut up and train before they find the way.

I was surprised to see him in his *keikogi zubon* (uniform bottoms) with only his *kuro obi* tied around his waste. His uniform top was slung over his shoulder and he directed me to find a place to sit in his home for a moment. Sitting and drinking out of a small square traditional wooden cup filled with cold *nigori sake* (potent *sake* fermented on the bottom of the bottle, as I learned later on), Sensei talked about *tameshiwari*. This word describes breaking techniques used in martial arts. I realized from his words and later from both experience, research, and study that this type of practice is used to overcome fear and to strengthen the human spirit and endurance. It is a useful means to test the power and effectiveness of one's personal *Budo* and is mandatory to win the battle of darkness within the inner self, so light will shine brightly.

Tameshiwari as found in the world of *kenjitsu* (sword art) is known as *tameshigiri,* or sword cutting. In the life of the *samurai,* the practice of cutting specially prepared and wrapped bands of straw reeds tested the cutting worthiness of the sword and strengthened the cuts themselves, which are the same cuts used in mortal combat. The ultimate significance of *tameshiwari* practice is the pure discipline of one's powers of concentration through physical action.

A famous thirteenth-century general named Hojo Tokiyoru, who became a priest in his later days, clearly revealed the most profound meaning of *tameshiwari*—that it crashed the mirror of long discipline and revealed *satori*. The board, brick, or tile that received the blow does not actually exist; the real object of the strike is oneself.

This single blow is what may be termed active meditation or *dozen*. In a sense, this is the actual means that most *Budoka* express in their daily practice and training. It is through this action that one must excel to the highest level of purity and high moral tones of individual responsibility as one demands human victory. The action of the break itself is a natural connection to the other side. It is a means to find pure and total *mushin,* or no-mind. It is a moment to blend and become the universal gathering of harmony at the rudimentary level.

Sensei began, "Today, Jack-*san,* you are going to assist me in a very special cinderblock *tameshiwari,* one which few have ever witnessed over the years. I will have some photos taken for future reference and you are to receive one as my gift." Later that year I did receive not only the photo to remember, but the negative as well to safely guard. Sensei's photographer friend was there too. Following Sensei, we passed through the house and into an entranceway to the basement of the old-style inner-city dwelling. We began our descent.

I had the feeling I was entering an ancient chasm—one in which I would face more of the same tests of courage and universal willpower. Descending the dark stairs, I recalled the ancient wisdom of the masters who taught the moral precept of *karate-do* and embraced the simple reality of shunning ego-centered distractions and inner conflict. I understood from Sensei that the cornerstone of martial arts was humility, which held the archaic fighting traditions in firm resolve. Virtue was fostered in *karate-do,* beyond all forms of vice. Sensei was in every sense an icon among all others who once trained when it was convenient. My *sensei* trained always as a moral means to face the austere obstructions found during the course of one's lifetime.

I often felt that Sensei must be a reincarnated priest of the Kashima and Kanori Shrines in the Hatachi Province or else Miyamoto Mushashi himself. All I knew was that I now found myself traveling full speed along the traditional boundless highway of precise *karate-do* transmission. Each step brought me closer to the source; the timeless realization of self-discovery was at every corner and in every special experience.

Deeper into the lower level we traversed. Sensei wore his clogs—

the traditional footwear in Japan—and his *keikogi,* and I wore my street clothes. The photographer was directly behind me, stumbling with his equipment each step of the way. Finding our way to the back of the basement, we reached an area with cinderblocks. A light illuminated the darkness in the corner of the world where only I and two others stood for a moment in time. Time seemed to stop.

There I was told to pass the large cinderblocks to Sensei as he stacked them, one atop the other. Two bricks served as a base. I had figured Sensei was going to show me a breaking technique used to build my spiritual strength, but no, he was planning to break the blocks himself, to scale the impossible peak.

As I picked each one up, and passed it to him, he seemed to make a chanting sound or breathing rhythm hardly audible to anyone a distance away. I assumed he was somehow preparing for the feat to come. Each pass of the block brought him closer to the goal he was to achieve. Some may think that breaking several boards, cement blocks, or a tower of frozen ice is a monumental achievement; I delivered fifteen slabs of concrete to the hands of Sensei before he motioned for me to stop, and that was only because we were out of materials. The barely audible sound he had been making ceased. Sounds or words used in tasks by *Budoka* were often repeated as a means to foster mental strength and pre-heat the *ki*. I used many sounds of the same origin myself in the form of affirmations directly related to the deep teachings of the *Bugei* (old martial arts) in the training of the subconscious.

I stepped back and stared as my eyes widened not only because of the magnitude of this stack, but because there were no spacers between them, which meant no air or give in any way to foster an easier break. This was the brutal force known to only those who witnessed it. The top block was about thirty inches off the ground and looked as unconquerable as a mountain of granite. Surrounding the enormous stack were other broken cinderblocks, house bricks, a wooden pile of broken boards, and amazingly enough, field stones all in rubble. To be exact, his basement looked like an odd quarry for various crushed stones.

The time drew near. I wondered about the years of extreme discipline and realized how austerity must become a way of life born of courage as the door to one's future. The gallant must learn to hold their heads high, maintain an unwavering course, and set their sails for a predetermined destiny. We learn to create our karma by our diligent focus as our practice becomes the vital medium to unlock our fears while we collect our knowledge to find peace.

The photographer set up his equipment for the feat about to unfold as I helped gather and remove various articles in the way. Sensei began to breathe deep using *fukoshuki-kokyu* (abdominal breathing), then *sanchin* (deep breathing) began. The lower level of the house began to roar with the grinding sound as Sensei unwound his innermost strength of *ki*. Wave after wave of deep breathing echoed from wall to wall, drawing me into the esoteric regions of my own mind. Another amazing ritual of Japan was mysteriously becoming real in every sense, yet it was still unknown to so many. This was *karate-do,* this was the secret of universal success, the connection between then and now, and the excitement of the true *Budo* in the making. With each breath, Sensei seemed to radiate greater power.

I could almost sense something inhuman intensifying the air, now seemingly timeless from his powerful *sanchin*. The rasp of his distinct voice seemed to draw me into a magical trance and then he moved toward the stack.

This was not simply mind over matter, this was the culmination of years of one-man *makiwara* over hundreds of thousands of times in the severe battles of human endurance and existence. Sensei moved to face the concrete monolith, poised and now still in concentration. The air was motionless. It was if Sensei Frost himself waited for an ancient intruder to appear from the sidelines to do mortal battle. The hair on the back of my neck stood up, perhaps from the eyes of other ancient *samurai* now standing in the shadows of the darkened basement where light died and emptiness remained. It was Sensei whose sword glistened in his hand as well and his armor *(yoroi)* that challenged any opposition. His armor was beyond all doubts his essence.

I stood motionless as the photographer readied himself with lights and multiple electronic gadgetry, hoping to catch the ultimate *tameshi-wari* of a lifetime.

Sensei placed the blade of his right hand upon the top block as if to offer condolences to the end of its life. His hand was massive in size from the months of *makiwara* practice in preparation for this quest. The knife edge of his hand was roughly callused and looked as though he had chipped away at it with a woodcarver's chiseling tool. The culmination of thousands of repetitions became the spearhead in force as he manifested to be unemotional and silent, as if he too were carved out of granite.

Long moments passed before he again moved his weapon into the air high above his head. Holding it a second, he brought it down against the mother lode at moderate speed, then ground the blade into the top block as if to taunt nature and the elements standing against him. Twisting his hand, he drew it high once again, holding the left palm out over the top slab as if to feel its aura. He held it motionless as if frozen in time. With a self-possessed spirit in a world of mortal combat, nothing mattered, only the action.

The samurai Bunojo stepped toward the path leading into the woods, casually passing a signpost which read "Yamato twenty miles." He had just slain the village fencing teacher during a duel. The teacher had publicly sworn to be invincible, announcing the challenge to any worthy opponent. In his black hakama and zori (sandals), Bunojo now stepped into the forest. Worn stepping stones formed the road to other cities, and ahead lay Yamato as he calmly moved deeper into the wood. The sun streamed through the tall Japanese pine trees, casting shadows while layer upon layer of multiple rays refracted the dense, humid, morning air.

Various moths and insects flew and danced in the warming drafts of the rising heat as they sought higher protection and sanctuary. A large native eagle flew through the treetops as if to warn Bunojo of evil and danger looming in the thicket.

Stepping out from the darkness were nine assassins who vowed to avenge their teacher. First one, then three, then all nine lined the path in front of him, drawing their swords in unison and challenging his mighty victory over the slain fencing master. Some Tokugawa bushi and students had come to avenge their master's honor. The leader held his position and shouted, "You dishonored our master and you dishonored our dojo, and now you will pay for your disrespect."

Bunojo answered back, "Your master was rude and flaunted his ability. He challenged all comers without the regard to bushido or for the humble forgiveness of Buddha's hand at my mastery. He paid for his short temper and lack of universal ability—I defeated not a teacher, but a child who used his mouth and one victory as his backbone. The duel was fair, as was the destiny of two samurai in time. You have no grudge with me."

"We will regain his honor and ours with our blood oath—kappan."
The first samurai kiaid and attacked with the thrust, but Bunojo simply sidestepped and cut his arm off with a diagonal slash. The samurai went screaming "Eeii!" into the woods, holding his arm as the blood sprayed. His severed hand and forearm lay along the side of the path.

Bunojo then stopped and held his position as still as the peaceful night, pulling his katana close to his face as if dreaming of another time, frozen in the broken stillness. Detached in the moment, the second and third samurai attacked with kiais screaming through the forest. Full speed up the cobblestone path they lunged. Both samurai attacked on forty-five-degree angles, slicing at his flanks. He broke his dead calm position and stepped through them as their swords chased open air, missing any mark. Within the midst of his movement he deflected one of the swords and horizontally cut the samurai's midsection. Turning in one motion he vertically cut the other samurai's backbone in a single stroke. Both stricken samurai stood motionless for a instant leaning against one another as they collided, then fell to earth in a shower of silent blood, death written across their faces.

Spinning back to the front, Bunojo once again began his journey as though on a soundless meditation quest. Slowly stepping one foot in front of the next, he now carried his katana out to his side. His other hand rested in the lapel of his uwagi above his hakama. His solitude was unbreakable, his demeanor stoically beautiful, as he seemed possessed by the gods. Moving ever so slowly, the next three samurai cautiously approached.

Three more warriors now centered themselves strategically in the road. The center bushi attacked ferociously, whipping his katana in large circular motions, then stopped in his tracks as Bunojo used the pear splitter by cleaving the enemy's body down the center from head to midsection. A fine, deep slash with a line of blood ran down his forehead, face, and chest, ending at his belly where the flow of crimson streamed uncontrollably outward. The samurai's stroke found a confused moth in the air, then his life ended. Bunojo stepped to the side casually as the samurai dropped spinning to the ground in a heap.

The other two hesitated, jockeyed for a safer position, stepped back and exchanged unruly words and attacked. First one, then the other followed. As one slipped by, Bunojo struck out powerfully with a diagonal cut from his attacker's left hip to his upper right chest. The other samurai thrust at Bunojo's neck, but Bunojo moved in time for the thrust to miss him and connect with his partner already dead in his tracks. Both fell to the earth gushing blood, lifeless for all eternity.

Of the three assassins left, two ran in horror, and the last one stood his ground a distance from Bunojo. Positioned in an upright almost casual stance, his katana still remained in its saya (scabbard). This was one of the older senior retainers to the fencing master. Poised and still he stood. The sun streamed rays of light through a break in the tall pine forest. A great white owl sat high above, watching the engagement. The senior fencing student stood motionless as Bunojo approached the opening in the path. Bunojo now with his katana back in its saya stepped forward until both seasoned samurai stood face to face.

Both stood composed and silent as if there were no conflict, no battle present. Only the sound of a soft wind blew through the pine tree tops, as needles dropped to the ground beside them. It was as if the forest was no longer separate from the two samurai left standing, as if all became immersed in the brutal yet beautiful conflict. Both stared distantly into each other's eyes as if nothing inside existed. No words or actions drew from their existence, only the ruffle of the air against their hakama as their lives drifted into a sea of nothingness.

It would be a speed draw (iaijittsu). The silence broke. Slowly Bunojo spoke, "I will see you in another time, samurai."

"You will see me in hell, Bunojo."

It was tachiojo (to die standing on your feet). Both would possibly die, but one would die first, the winner last. Moments passed before the samurai technique and ritual known as aiuchi (mutual slaying) would be executed.

An eagle screamed from high above, and a feather drifted down through the air to meet the men. The retainer drew his lightning katana instantly, but before it could clear the saya, Bunojo had charged in a final breath toward his opponent and drew his katana with a reverse hand, horizontally slicing his opponent through his drawing arm, then across the heart, and as if nothing occurred, divided the drifting feather in two before it touched the ground with another instant horizontal cut.

A shower of blood flew from the retainer's chest as his face and eyes expressed the horror of surprise. No one had ever beaten him before. Bunojo stood in a deep stance, his stricken opponent behind him, and focused his eyes on the blade of his katana, which reflected and mirrored the retainer dropping to the ground behind his heels. Words slipped from his mouth as his katana glistened with blood, "Yamato is waiting."

Samurai Bunojo shook the blood from his katana, replaced it delicately into its saya, and dusted himself off. Walking down the road his shoulders snapped back in proud fashion as he headed for the ancient town. Behind him lay seven excellent warriors, soon to be forgotten.

Sensei drew in his breath slowly and deeply and with a smooth controlled exhale sound in his throat, he slammed moderately against the top brick, ground the blade of his knife hand into the cement once again and then drew his hand upward. Out of his mouth came the words *zenbu no ki*—"the force of *ki* altogether in one single blow." He would break on the third strike. Twice now, lights flashed as he struck the top block in preparation, and now in three more thrusts he would attempt to conquer the entire *samurai* spirit.

Down he came once again—slam!—and then once more. We readied ourselves and our excited spirits. Sensei seemed powerful in his lasts moments, his *keikogi* damp and his chest steaming with magnificent deliverance. He inhaled deeply, and in a rush of magic wind a *kiai* with the spirit of a thousand warriors rang out in a charge.

His body seemed to lift itself into the air as his arm and knife hand cut through time and moment in one blinding fury. As he slammed full power into the top block, a tidal wave of shock drove through the entire stack. It was as if I were watching history unfold in a master plan known only by the ancients. Bits and pieces of cement flew everywhere, the flashes riveted the darkness, and the entire stack came crashing to the floor in an uncontested explosion.

It was magnificent! The photos were made and the precise timing could not have been better. Now, I could only hope for the safety of the photographer if the development of the film were poor. We would have to wait. I celebrated Sensei's victory and expressed great honor for having witnessed his unbeatable task.

"Jack-*san*, please grab me a wet towel and pack it full of ice. I believe I may have broken my hand."

"*Hai,* Sensei," I responded. I ran full speed up the stairs to the ice box and fetched the ice, then a towel. Arriving back down below, I found Sensei pleased although I knew he was in pain. Stoic and proud, the ordeal of his attainment overshadowed the most grueling pain. This was the way in *Budo.*

Sensei shoved his hand into the wet towed filled with ice and spoke of his focus and what he needed to work on. I, of course, was still in awe, unable to express my opinion because there was no more to be said. He did it and no one else ever has to this day. I started to clean up, but Sensei told me to leave everything so more photos could be shot. I stayed for *sake,* beer, and more talk as the day wore on. So as not to be rude, I carefully asked Sensei if there was anything else I could do for his injury before I headed homeward.

"No, *domo,* Jack-*san.* You go and consider what you witnessed today and I will see you later on."

It wasn't until the next day that I received more information about the photos taken. The results weren't all good news, to say the least, but the most important photo did turn out—the one I still have today. It remains in my vault, safe from decay just so I can look at it every once in a while. It caught Sensei right at the time of the break, "A warrior facing the Universe."

The exact moment where the results of *ki* are transformed into explosive universal strength had materialized. What is kept inside and transformed into useful energy is known as the will *(kokorozashi).* When this will is transformed outside the body, it becomes the intrinsic *ki.* The will and the *ki* are closely related and generally the same, so the will or mind must be corrected and made right, so that right action will follow. When all is in perfect accord, we find the pinnacle of harmony and that which is clear.

The resulting action of all these factors in beautiful balance forges happiness, and peace in the self. As mentioned earlier, this feeling found in life as one succeeds or achieves intense moments of great triumph is known as the remaining spirit, or *zanshin*. Strive to find the beautiful realization *(zanshin)* and use it as a means to transport oneself to the foremost measure of tranquility. Training in the *Budo* must become the way. That is, the way of the peaceful warrior in life itself.

I dreamed of the event for weeks, and wondered what the future held for me. I allowed my mind to respond, *Just keep training, Jacksan, and never lose heart.* I heard my enduring Sensei repeat this mantra.

Ki—Spirit

CHAPTER TWELVE

The New South Wales Incident

Makiwara practice had taken my whole morning and my intention was to build a strong fighting spirit. *Makiwara* (striking post) literally means "straw sheath" and was used as an intense training tool in the Ryukyu Islands of southern Japan. *Makiwara* was emphasized by the great Master Kanryo Higashionna (1853–1916), *sensei* of the *Naha-te* style of self-defense. *Makiwara* was passed along to many students, including Chojun Miyagi, the student of Higashionna Sensei and founder of the *Gojo-Ryu* system. *Makiwara* was a predominant training aspect of many Okinawan and Chinese *kempo* systems. *Makiwara* was highly emphasized and characterized by Sensei Brian Frost, my teacher of *Koei-Kan karate-do.* I too learned to strengthen the body and mind as one through *makiwara.*

I stood in front of the *makiwara* as though a war had begun. I faced all odds, willing to make a total sacrifice. Two thousand repetitions was the number—stroke by stroke. I finished my punching routine and switched automatically without missing a beat into my sword hand strikes. The harmonious cadence of each movement drove me deeper into the disposition of survival and the warrior mind.

Four thousand repetitions among fist, elbow, and foot techniques prepared me for the next training challenge in the heart of the *karate-do* academy. Along with *makiwara,* I was consumed with the science of *kotekitai* (body toughening). This type of practice prepares one for the mental and physical demands and hardships faced during fighting and in life's ordeals. Pairing off with my junior student, I demanded he attack me over and over again with specific kicking methods while I pounded my arms against his aggression in the struggle to toughen my forearms and temper my body and mind for battle. This is known as arm pounding. The words *seishin tanren* were repeated in my mind until I lost track of time. *Seishin tanren* (spirit forging) tempered and shaped my arsenal before and during actual engagement. Pushing forward, I quickly changed students in order to keep the pressure on and gain all that I could in a limited time frame. "More power. Harder! Harder!" I shouted.

With each thundering kick and punch, I forced my training opponent to fall in exhaustion, only to find another to take his place. Next, I accepted body blows from both kicks and punches without any blocks at all. These continuous attacks were directed at specific areas of the body. Torso, rib cage, stomach, chest, and back were pummeled until you fell under the exhaustion of the practice and failure of body resistance. It seemed to be something of the teacher's quest—to see his students break in battle long before he himself demonstrated any limitations or imperfections of spirit or body.

In real *Budo,* one needs to understand the difference between half-truths and half-lies. One must become forthright and completely sincere. This is termed *seijin.* There is a Japanese phrase, *tatemae no honne* which means facade vs. reality. The Japanese concern with interpersonal harmony led to the development of a system of behavior that included careful control of facial expressions and body movements. This highly stylized form of communication was designed to avoid misunderstanding of any kind in social situations. In essence, the Japanese created two worlds, one of reality, or *honne,* which were the true thoughts and intentions, and one of facade or *tatemae,* which projected a screen or a manner of harmony that could constitute a ploy.

The Japanese used this system to do business and win in the game of strategy and tactics. The shielding of emotions and feelings or what the Japanese term self-control was used to create an illusion of various manners in order to satisfy an end. This type of practice was expressed in a ritualized way to succeed in any endeavor. Therefore, in Japan, one was ridiculed when mere calculation or logic was implemented without this type of specialized tactic.

In *Budo,* you are taught the best use of *honne,* as it is beneath the *Budoka* to lie or cheat in his intentions. Honesty and courtesy were two of the many virtues one was required to cultivate to obtain enlightenment. Only in an actual battle engagement was the *tatemae* presented in a more formidable way. In *senso*-battle, if one were to project one's true intentions, then failure would ensue. The study of *tatemae no honne* is very important to develop a means to win.

Three hours passed before the exercise was finished and I could take time to focus on the business of running the *dojo.* Standing outside in the warm sun gave me a fresh breath of life and reassurance of my endurance. I watched the cars passing by, knowing full well that few of their occupants would ever understand what *Budo* was really about. Such was life. Perhaps others employed a different means to achieve the same end.

Stepping back into the *dojo* sent me back in time, back to the land of the legendary *samurai.* I had placed all my ancient photos and records of important historical data in strategic locations to encourage fighting spirit in the purist manner. In Chinese, this is called *feng shui,* or the art of placement. A master of *feng shui* is one who can design and place objects in a particular way to affect the spirit of anyone entering the area. True ability need not be displayed or flaunted to express the essence of one with great knowledge. It can be sensed in peculiar ways. A true *Budoka* comes to understand this truth.

Recognition of those who came before and the lineage of those who remain loyal to the cause of self-development in my system was enhanced by photos that hung from the wall in the foyer *(genkan)* and office *(jimushu).* One had a feeling of being back in the Orient, in Nippon or Okinawa, and this recreated element helped to bring one closer to the essentials of *Budo.*

Glossy light-colored hardwood floors surrounded the *taijo* and *tatami,* where the training of warriors took place day in and day out. Twelve sets of full contact armor were positioned on the wall around the *taijo*. These were used to test your courage in battle to the fullest extent possible. Use of this armor allowed you to focus battle in its truest sense and come to understand your potential without placing yourself in mortal danger. Worthy of its purpose, the armor forced you to battle in the most formidable way—ultimate full-contact warfare. With this type of practice, you are able, as the *Nihonjin* say, to show your stomach, or *hara wo miseru*. Taking a chance was not only common but was in fact expected in full-contact fighting. Actually, this expression refers more to the fact of being completely honest or opening up, as in a heart-to-heart talk. You can be *hara wo miseru* to yourself in combative reality.

The surroundings weren't there to be observed, they were there to be utilized in the most demanding manner. Each practice aid was a specialized tool whose function chipped away at the rough edges. The honing of skills became the mainstay of daily living while using the ancient methods of hard-line *Budo* practice. *Ningen wa, shinu mono da* (man is mortal) is completely true, but his nature can be transformed into an intimidating weapon like a sword that saves life, or one that usurps the evil found in life.

I was pleased with this West Coast *dojo*. I heard a couple of voices in the lobby as I stood on the *tatami*. Entering the *genkan*, I approached two men who stood waiting for an introduction. Richard and Donald were their names, both responding with a type of Gaelic accent. Many a *karateka* had entered my *dojo* in the hopes of testing skills against me and challenging the system I promoted. Once again, on an ordinary day in June, the responsibility of representing a combative system rested on my shoulders. I didn't yet realize that the Koei-Kan *karate-do* "heart" would be revealed in its truest nature.

Richard, a lean, stocky, and muscular man, did most of the talking. He spoke in some detail. "We have been touring the West Coast, going from school to school requesting permission to practice with students and gather knowledge about their expertise. Both of us practice *Wado-Ryu* in New South Wales, and run *dojo*s there. I am a *sandan* [third-degree black belt] and Donald here is a *nidan* [second-degree black belt]. Actually, we spend a lot of time practicing *kumite* as a specialty in our *dojo*s and want to increase our skills before we go back. Your *dojo* is the last on our list to inspect, so before we leave for home tomorrow, it was our hope to practice with you."

"Be our guests," I answered. "Our class is tonight at six o'clock and afterward we can go through some *kumite*. There is a specific type of fighting we do which incorporates the use of the wall in a way one can rarely escape and must defend oneself. I'll explain it to you later, so if you are still interested, you can join in with some of my juniors or myself."

I knew that a test of their expertise would be in the plan for me that night, so placing them in a class would give me a chance to observe their conditioning and skill before any full-blown contact battle ensued. It was customary in the days of the *samurai* to have a new-comer's skill *(tegiwa)* tested by junior students or a senior before the head instructor unleashed his expertise. I followed that tradition most of the time, depending on my mood.

Donald, who stood about six feet tall, didn't say too much. He just sort of nodded his head in affirmation of what his companion said and stood silent. Sometimes the quiet ones hold the most surprises. I expected nothing, but anticipated everything. In any case, I hoped the new visitors would allow me the liberty to cast my hammer upon the anvil to reinforce my *seishin*.

Richard said, "I have been into kickboxing for over three years and training in *Wado-Ryu* for about twelve years. I enjoy kickboxing more because it allows me to express the power of my art to the fullest without a bunch of rules and regulations."

I rarely found a kickboxer who offered much in the way of new knowledge. It was always the same—punch, jab, slop kick—over and over again. Many of the kickboxers I had met had an illusion of grandeur and fame. In the long run, however, they ended up frustrated and unsatisfied because their chosen art lacked the character found in traditional *Budo*, or the challenge of combative reality backed with ancient throws and grappling *(katame waza)*.

The hidden secrets *(okuden)* found in the ancient martial arts are seldom disclosed until after years of loyalty. Much of kickboxing offers what may be called the quick fix, but after the application of boxing strategy becomes mundane, most students end up feeling disenchanted.

However, every pugilist, every *karateka,* and every *Budoka* must find his own way and conquer his own particular fears. It's truly the emotion of fear which sets into motion our negative or destructive attitudes. In the process of rising to the challenge of one's martial art, the reality of any combat is to know thyself, to understand that which is difficult to find—one's essence. A Japanese proverb, *Kyo wa ki wo utsu* ("Your place of abode directs your spirit"), teaches us that humans are often affected by the condition of their surroundings. The *dojo* which had become my home away from home was designed and constructed to foster a strong bond to the teachings of *Budo* based on the virtues of understanding and compassion. The *dojo* or "Way place,"reveals a hidden substance to find the self through time and becomes the sanctuary of truth and sincerity—*seijin.* Tonight I hoped to find some of that truth in combat.

Shortly after meeting the two Australians, I left for lunch at the local Japanese restaurant. Lunch was a unique lesson in speaking a foreign language which fueled my mind culturally before going back to the *dojo.* Each weekday afternoon, I would speak *Nihongo* and practice *tetsugaku* (philosophy) to observe and absorb the delicate manners *(saho)* and ways of the Japanese. Japanese philosophy and psychology, manifested in their arts, crafts, and lifestyle, created one of the most admirable cultures ever devised. On the other hand, it has an inhumane characteristic too. This aspect stifles the individuality and creativity of the Japanese and holds them in harsh bondage to the state. Japanese are always in fear of making mistakes or offending someone; they dread creating a controversy. From my contact with them, I learned the importance of their type of communication and the meaning of *enryo* (holding back).

During my time in Japan, I had discovered at first that this simply means to shut up. As I trained with my *sensei* in Detroit I learned two distinct sayings: "You do not quit" and "Shut up and train." So during my learning, I went one step further and made a point to focus on the old *Budo*-style language, which is difficult to find, let alone understand. This complex language, called *heigo,* was in many ways transmitted to me by my *sensei* directly and informally by letter, as distinctly different from the *kotoba* (standard language of communication). In much of the *Budo* style, there are many *koto waza* or proverbs and sayings which provide a more ancient way of transmitting a meaning in the *Nihongo* body language. A nation is able to mirror its thinking by this manner of communication. In a sense, it becomes part of the ritual found and practiced by the martial artist.

One following the Japanese Way has to become sensitive and receptive to the form, process, and nuances of Japanese etiquette in order to achieve true knowledge. These things must be wanted and cultivated in order to see through the cultural walls that create a facade during the learning journey. This is an ancient understanding most *karateka* never learn or research. Physical techniques are the pinnacle most reach.

In *Budo* the bond between the *sensei* and student, master and disciple, is ideally so close that the central core of most teachings is passed on through *haragei.* This term is used to connote the learning of technique not only through explicit instruction, but through the unconscious imitation of the teacher. You begin as an apprentice, and as you become proficient and master the skills, you develop *kizuna,* or ties/bonds, to the teacher. The practice of *Budo* fosters great loyalty and bridges the gaps which hide fears and misunderstandings. *Chugi* (loyalty) is by far one of the most important virtues of the teacher-student relationship. You learn from the very beginning that the *sensei* leads as a benevolent dictator, not compromising his belief system, but allowing you to adapt in relation to both your personal needs and the *sensei's* demands in accordance with the *do* (way). You learn that the *sensei* is accorded respect due not to any social prestige he may enjoy outside the *dojo,* but to the very skills he demonstrates within the *dojo.*

Leaving the restaurant, my mind slipped into its meditative state, where I think as I move, concentrate on one task as I do another. *Step after step,* I thought, *boxing, kickboxing, he focuses on points or the one KO punch. He jabs and punches, slips and counters, and hopes to win by sport.* In our *Budo,* we win by the art of deception, the bare-knuckled approach to battle, and the attacking of vulnerable areas called *kyushu. Kyushu* are the sensitive striking areas found on the body that determine life and death via the right focused blow.

Hooks, upper cuts, and short weak kicks of various degrees usually come from kickboxers. My defense will entail elbows on the inside, knees, and sweeps. I will use him as an example to demonstrate the combative skills found in a warrior's mind, set on destroying the enemy's spirit. I outlined the tactics I would use. Most *karateka* use the basic means to defend and attack; I go one step further. My fists had been tempered to extreme hardness with salt brine and *makiwara,* my shins conditioned by sandbags and shin-pounding techniques. I knew that if my opponent seemed formidable, I would simply crush his guard, thus his mind and spirit, by first blasting his fist with my own. I knew that if I tied up with him, I would use my elbows to smash his guard and take him to the ground. My preparation of battle was a shrewd test, a mind game of tactics and strategy found in warfare.

I walked down the boulevard toward the front of my proud *dojo.* The streets were lined with palm trees hanging still in the afternoon air. I used to punch anything to temper my hands: trees, walls, buses. But now I had the *makiwara,* where I would spend the rest of the day in physical meditation unleashing every conceivable striking technique in anticipation for the exciting evening quest. I needed to smash my inflated yet uncertain ego and renew my honorable intentions as an example to my students on the field of honor. The evening would soon fall upon me and the events would open the door of extreme experience for all who participated. I entered my quiet *dojo.* In the *taijo,* I gazed into the solitude of the afternoon stillness. The time had come to meditate, and so briefly, I did.

Intense conditioning was the focus of group class, scheduled to begin around six o'clock. I prepared to hold the gathering of all warriors' minds and hearts. Class was a test of endurance, and a series of attacking or defensive movements set in an unrelenting cadence to shape and cultivate the fighting spirit of the entire student body. Here on common ground, *Budoka* forced themselves through the ordeals and grueling pain of attempting to make it successfully through the last technique at any cost, or risk losing face dropping out early.

That evening, as usual, the students began to line up according to rank: the black belts to the right followed by brown belts and lower ranks methodically in proper order. I left the training hall for a glimpse of the sun setting in the west toward Nippon. Colors ran across the sky as the sun dropped into the big blue. My Japanese garden near the front door was flourishing. Entering this *dojo* was an escape back in time to a land and culture that charged my spirit. I felt the passion of *Budo,* the awakening of my insides as excitement built from the expectation of a special hard-line class, and the hopes of sharpening my combative skills.

Out of the corner of my eye I saw two figures approaching the camp, two travelers on a campaign in search of enlightenment. I thought to myself, "You shall see the light in the darkness tonight, my friends." Stepping back into the *dojo* as though I didn't notice them, I lined everyone up. About forty students stood at full attention in preparation for the physical tasks about to begin. I turned to see the two guests standing in the entranceway. Greeting them, I told them to go into the locker room, change, then stretch before entering class.

"Are we to go to class?" Richard asked.

I answered, "Class is mainly a warm-up before we begin free-sparring or any type of contact that is of a combative nature. You're in shape for a warm-up, aren't you?"

Richard answered, "By all means."

"Good, then we shouldn't be more than a short hour before we get down to business." I wondered about their condition.

Class began after a brief discourse on our search for *Budo* enlightenment. The heavy-duty cadence of class was relentless tonight. I noticed many seniors forcing themselves diligently to maintain the right mindset and make it through, catching their breath and at times gagging to hold their guts. Thirty minutes into the class and the two guests were faltering considerably with each step. The *kiais* were strong and echoed through the *dojo* into the alley where a couple of spectators observed through the back door. In front, a couple of street punks drifted in, took a look, and quickly slithered back out in the streets with other friends, feeling more sure of themselves there. In the *dojo,* reality struck them in the face and sent them clamoring to safer ground.

Once again, my honored guests began to falter and in one moment fell off to the side into exhaustion. I motioned them to fall into the back row where they could drop out from time to time without disturbing the class. This was the first lesson in humility. Everyone stood at attention catching their wind and regrouping their minds. *Seishin* (spirit) ran high as the more seasoned black belts forced themselves brutally onward, where juniors hesitated and fought with their emotions. The two guests now stood toward the back with beginners (no doubt with frustration) as they lost face from their weak spirits. I found out in those last moments just how solid their hearts were. I pushed forward in the hopes of extracting a few more of my warriors who stood in testimony to their excellent condition. All remained with the exception of a few white belts. The visitors now fell out completely and were sitting on the sidelines.

I decided to end class quickly rather than go the entire march, so once again, I had all the students regroup, catch their wind, and prepare for *kumite* (free-sparring). My final words were short and honorable concerning philosophical views. I announced that we had two martial arts technicians from New South Wales who were traveling the United States visiting *dojo*s in order to increase their expertise in *karate-do.* "This *dojo* will do what it can to meet their needs," I said. Inside, it was quite a different matter. I thought of the discipline I would impart upon these two traveling Spartans, and the memories of battle moments left for future recall in the corners of their martial minds.

I directed all those involved in free-sparring to gather their contact equipment and prepare for what was to come. Intermediate and advanced students made their way to the locker room for skimpy forearm pads, shinpads, and mouthpieces used normally during full contact in the *dojo.* They all found a place on the *tatami,* sat, and began to tape old injuries and reinforce weak areas that needed to be protected during *kumite* engagement. Students scattered here and there, outside the front door, and went through the ritual of mind and body preparation prior to the coming ordeal. I grabbed a roll of tape in my office and wrapped my left hand, damaged repeatedly after my last contact session with several of my black belts during *nage* (throwing practice). In traditional *judo,* practitioners used *nage* like I do *maki-wara.* To the tune of thousands of repetitions, *judoka* throw their partners one after another without hesitating to test their *ki* and connect with *Budo.* This ritualized self-defense martial arts form is the very child of the time-honored martial art of *jujitsu* systems used in individual one-to-one combat.

In our system of *karate-do,* we use a unique form of training to temper the student and test the extreme of human will. This is called *shomen kabe-kumite,* fighting against the main wall of the *dojo.* Another word for this is related to some ancient Okinawan *kata*s called *nai-hanchi,* fighting holding the ground. Its purpose is to have one opponent stand with his back to the wall, allowed to move sideways or slightly forward, to block and counter, but unable to escape or initiate the attack. With this complication, the defender has limited options and could be easily destroyed by an aggressive, top-ranked, conditioned fighter. Defense is greatly enhanced with this type of battle practice and allows one to become fearless in his mind. Solidification of mind and body is essential if one is to see the way. Endurance based on continued hardening of the body allows fear to become a fleeting thought instead of an insurmountable obstacle.

The attacker has the option to initiate attacks, create stratagems, find weaknesses, and smash his adversary in the traditional manner. In this exercise, the attacker uses tactics to unnerve his opponent, and unlimited use of striking, grappling, and throwing techniques is incorporated. Being smashed against the wall or thrown into it is not an unusual tactic. Often this extreme measure of warfare becomes the safest place to be while inside a bar or engaged in battle in tight quarters. It eventually becomes comforting.

Original battle consisted of finding the most awkward situation and looking for a way out. Too many conditions based upon regulations and rules were exactly the opposite of what occurs in street battle. Primitive engagement allows the Spartans to duel using whatever means possible to survive and emerge victorious. Seek the unexpected, deliver the most disturbing tactics to throw the enemy into chaos. Use expertise in *heiho* to confuse and then gain victory. Win the battle before you engage. Win in your mind first.

You could say that *kabe-kumite* is one of the most grueling forms of battle, as wave after wave of student is pitted against the defender until he falls victim or becomes invincible and unyielding. This challenging aspect of battle hones, polishes, and tempers the *bujin* to the mastery of the mind and one's universal energy. The warrior cannot be skilled in everything, but he can be skilled in his own level of excellence. In the final analysis, courage makes the man, and it is courage that shows one the light in the face of adversity. A coward turns away, but a brave man chooses danger and risk. Risk is the forerunner of championship in real life.

I motioned for all the practicing *Budoka,* now prepared to do *kumite,* to line up on the wall with partners. They formed groups of three or four, one with his back against the wall who would act as defender using counterattacking, and one on the outside facing his opponent using *seme,* or attacking methods. The others in each group would stand fast watching, preparing strategy for his turn as attacker. Each round would last three minutes, until exhaustion transpires or the exercise ends.

Donald was put with a group of one black belt and two brown belts. These brown belts were tough and loved the art of contact. Soon, they would advance to the level of *shodan* (black belt) and represent the *dojo* in the highest of our honors.

I believed this grouping was a good idea since both of my brown belts were of the grappling type. Don was tall and lanky, had long arms for good reach, and would most likely use looping punches. Tall individuals usually inherit this characteristic and make excellent targets for those who get inside. It would also be good experience for my men since their advanced test was slated for late summer, in which the test of ultimate skill would be sought in the war to make first-degree black belt. That event would last an incredible five hours in the ultimate evaluation of human endurance.

Richard the kickboxer was grouped with one of my senior brown belts and a junior whom I knew was aggressive, since he came to the *dojo* with a championship wrestling title and experience in high school. The youngest of five brothers gets quite a beating as he grows up, learning from the school of hard knocks. Hungry as he was, Richard would be an exhausting handful for him. My senior brown belt was a triathlon competitor, a fireman, and champion contender in the fireman Olympics. He lived to remain in shape, to make his life an adventure of conditioning. I stepped back a while to execute commands over the practice and initiate some type of order during the onslaught. I intended to get my licks and experience in due time, but I was fast growing impatient.

The terms and conditions of the training practice were announced. "No limits on contact to the body, foot contact only to the head. Throws, sweeps, grappling are permitted and points for winning rounds will be called by the individuals in the group. Each round will last three minutes, then the defender against the wall will automatically rotate to the standing position and take one cycle off in which to rest."

So the scene was set, four groups of battle-weary and seasoned technicians primed to test their courage, to face whatever adversity lay before them and deal with it accordingly.

The wall had been covered with *tatami* standing upright. This acted as a buffer and cushion for shock as bodies slammed into them. Long ago, in an old *dojo* that I looked back to in memory, this same type of fighting was done without the protection of any mat. The walls in the old days were made of concrete block. Nothing protected one from the possibility of having his head smashed against it other than skill to win and survive. Nowadays, things were more elegant even in battle. More safety was required with the laws and the lawsuits now filed at every lack of responsibility. It was a time of taking "the easy way out."

The time was set on the clock for the first round to begin. Other junior students gathered around the main hall and found places to sit and observe the free-sparring. This was a time students found the chance to see their *sensei* in action and to experience the thrill and the mastery of contact in years to come. One gains much from observation. I allowed Richard and Donald to be attackers first, to see their range of motion, their expertise on the field of engagement, and to determine my own tactics. Each group bowed to my command, *"Rei,"* (bow), then *"Hajime."* (Begin.)

Three groups forced against the wall engaged in battle, moving from left to right, up and down, hammering the defender at all costs. Punches started flying, kicks thundered through the air, and *kiais* filled the *dojo* atmosphere as wave after wave of battle wore on. Bodies collided against the wall in a clash or one group fell over into another group's area, intermingling with their battle momentarily. It was an important reality to experience your defensive powers and control when you were trapped against other individuals or in a corner. All conditions were met as in a bar situation or an alley.

Two of the combatants found themselves on the floor grappling in all directions, until I instructed one of the seniors to break them apart. Back to the wall they went, first bowing in respect, then engaged in battle the next instant full force. Three minutes passed without any major injury or mishap. My wrestler and my senior brown belt finished a gruelling engagement, bowed to each other, then rotated to the end of the line.

Next, Brad the fireman was paired off with Richard the kickboxer. Down the line, Donald was paired off with one of my brown belts, who was tall and more seasoned in his expertise. Everyone held their new ground and caught their breath. Both of the *Wado-Ryu* boys were at a loss, since we normally do our *kumite* without gloves or contact protection of any kind. Most *karateka* today use bizarre manufactured contact equipment purchased from various suppliers. When one is clad in the assorted colors and shapes of this protective gear, he appears to be more of an alien being instead of a warrior bearing the formidable appearance of a *samurai.* Our standard rule was no protection unless you have an injury.

I knew the kickboxers were used to gloves and foot protection. They both looked at each other acknowledging our contact rules, then at me with an uncertainty in their eyes. Our practice consisted of *makiwara, tameshiwari* (breaking techniques), and hardening exercises, all of which tempered the striking surfaces of body weapons used in full battle. It seemed our visitors were momentarily set back with frozen nerves hidden behind a facade. Their sensitivity to this issue somehow made their doubts squeeze through. Victor or vanquished, what would be the conclusion?

I shouted once again, *"Rei, hajime!"* It was time to see the kickboxers on the defensive. All warriors moved in defiance of the odds and dodged various strikes and full-power thrusts. The *tatami* gave and buckled with thuds as each warrior smashed the wall with tempered bodies. Shouts of *kiai* filled the evening air, and formidable energies contracted in explosive displays of *samurai* in conflict.

Tensions rose as wave after wave of assaults were launched in successive barrages. Kicks were blocked, punches were absorbed and deflected, opponents locked in mortal combat shifted to use throws and fell to the *tatami* below. Like a pack of wolves attacking their prey, all fighting now became more aggressive as lungs seemed about to burst. I felt at ease and was in my bliss as the warfare continued.

Looking toward the conflicts down the wall, I noticed my brown belt taking the battle to Don. The tall, lanky, New South Wales boy was growing weary and tied up to catch his breath. I knew this was at the very least a bad move. Tying up and grappling was stepping into the lion's jaw and waiting for him to close his mouth. Tireless as if in mechanical pursuit, the nightmare of failure began unfolding for Don in a matter of seconds. He grabbed on to my brown belt student, now in an entangled grappling position, and I noticed elbows and knees fly loose. As they crashed into the corner where the matted wall met the mirrors, an elbow smashed into the kickboxer's ribs, then another, then knees smashed the quadriceps and chest as big Don hit the ground. Still not wise enough to throw in the towel, Don attempted to sweep the attacker's leg from a ground position and caught him in the side of the knee.

Once again, bad move. Reeling back to repeat the same move, my brown belt lifted his leg off the mats at the last moment and slammed his heel into the back of his opponent's rib cage. Don got the message and gave up, with frustrated emotions coming through. The *dojo* heated up from class and battle; the sweat from each opponent's body soaked his uniform. Don, now frustrated by rib damage and a foot injury while making contact, fell to the sidelines, demoralized. Pain filled his face as one of the junior students left to retrieve some ice packs from the first aid station. (The "first aid station" was the corner liquor store. The owners were accustomed to seeing students flock in every Tuesday and Thursday night to buy ice. They knew the dilemma of late-night action.)

Richard and my brown belt, Brad, now exchanged techniques in the expectation to score and win. With an iron will, Brad poured on the pressure. Brad had one of those blazing reverse punches that seemed to find its mark at the most unexpected time. The blaze raged on as each Spartan drove thundering weapons forward with tenacity and resolution. Jab, jab, jab, then a series of roundhouse kicks flew through the air, finding their targets but without penetration. Brad had the advantage of creating the opening by using years of strategy with bare knuckle expertise. This was his chance to expose his mastery of warfare on his own turf as he saw it and show others he was ready for the rank of *shodan*. As one of his front kicks landed and bounced off the forearm of Richard on the receiving end, a counterattack slammed Brad's midsection.

Instantaneously, Brad buckled under the surprise pressure of an upper cut to the floating rib. Unseen before it slammed in, the shock caught him off guard and blew the wind out of him. Brad covered his head to buy time and the kickboxer briefly let up and moved back to the wall in ready position. The clock's buzzer rang out and everyone stopped. I motioned Brad and Richard to continue and instructed others to rotate and begin again.

Once again Brad began his blitz to find victory. I could tell he was injured, but continued on. Brad forced combinations and landed a hook kick to the head, but Richard rebounded with two hook shots to the body, caught the midsection once again, and then Brad faltered, dropping his guard. Richard launched a thrust to the forehead with full power and connected to the upper eye without any consideration. Blood ran down Brad's face in streams, but he continued. I halted the match. Brad, now bristling with frustration and spotted with blood, had to quit. This looked bad for the *dojo,* just when he was doing so well fighting an individual with years on his sword and seasoned for cutting. The head shot was without merit, but they were in the heat of battle. I knew Richard deliberately laid open Brad's eye and robbed him of his ego. Such were the spoils of war. I stopped the engagement and walked over to inspect the wound. It appeared that it would call for seven or eight stitches, so I told Brad to go to emergency and have it taken care of. I knew it was worse.

I now had a reputation to stand up for, and casually glancing at the *Wado-Ryu* boy, I said, "All right, Richard, I suppose my boy is out of it for now, but you've only been working out for a few minutes, so I'll work with you and see what you've got." Other students could see my *ki* beginning to glow. I now had to take control and offer a solution to the dark blemish placed on our *dojo* by a stranger from a strange land. Any visitor who left this turf would have quite another story to tell when I finished with him, I assured myself.

All other battles had come to a halt. Only I and the kickboxer stood, two lone Spartans on the field of battle ready to win the war for our side. I chose to be the defender first and motioned the young warrior to exchange positions. I put my back to the green *tatami* wall, smashed my fists together, and took several deep abdominal breaths before we began. We both knew where this was going, and I, for one, was determined to end the battle. I figured I would feel him out, build his confidence, and then smash his ego like a bad habit. We bowed and took our positions, guard ready. I shouted to the time keeper to set the clock for thirty minutes.

Richard's eyes opened wide as I mentioned that I usually do one- to two-hour rounds with all my students. He snickered and said, "Oh, is that so, mate?" I blurted out, "Let's go." Circling, I moved to the right and the left, dropping my guard to draw him in, to entice him to foolishly fall into the trap of my tactics. I knew that now, if I could allow him enough rope to set himself up, he would eventually hang himself. The noose began to tighten right away. His eyes widened once again and then a series of jabs came in a barrage to set me up. I casually slapped them down and to the side only to move out of range while he attempted another attack.

The gathered students fell silent and the surrounding area became an endless black hall. My mind became more focused and the intensity of my inner energy seemed to grow as fuel was added to the fire. I sought to find enlightenment in the heat of battle. Time and breathing now began to blend into a calm state, a mind of nothingness.

He launched two hook kicks, I dodged them both, then a roundhouse kick entered my midsection. I allowed it to make contact without any effect to unnerve his mind. He followed with two hooks to the body and I countered. As he connected against my forearm (used as cover over my midsection), I launched a blazing hook to his head. Bang! I rattled his cerebrum. He faltered momentarily and got the best of his senses. Somewhat dazed, he turned his head to the side where a large red mark surfaced on his temple region. Though I now knew that I could deck this opponent in a furious attack, I held back to test him more, and to experiment with my *heiho*.

We both picked up the pace. Every time a kick was delivered to my body, he would systematically follow with hooks to the body or head. Never seeming to change his tactics, he was measured easily in both physical and mental strategy. This was expected of a boxer's mentality: the deliberate repetition of combinations used to score rather than destroy the enemy with one blow as in *karate-do*. I maintained the theory that this could be a facade for another tactic used in battle. The difference in our design was that he used kickboxing mentality, I used combative formulation. In true martial arts genius, anything is possible during warfare. The idea, of course, is to destroy the enemy without effort and to silently win with the "Art of Deception."

Next, a front kick came sizzling in to my midsection, but I swept left and grabbed the leg to throw him. He attempted to match my tactic and throw the opposite leg while I held on, but to no avail I dropped his leg the moment he let loose his other one, and down he went to the *tatami*. I followed up with a punch or two to his head on the mats, but quickly returned to the wall. We both knew what the final outcome would have been had I continued. One of the most common problems faced by martial artists is that if one does not forcibly finish an attack, no one can be sure that one really could have won. Did I or did he, could I or could he? Not good thoughts to maintain during battle.

Momentarily stopping, I motioned to switch positions in the exercise. I now became the attacker, where he became the defender. The stocky kickboxer gasped for air, heaved his chest, and wiped the sweat from his brow. I was now entirely warmed up. I became more intense in my manner, beginning to unleash powers I usually held back. Students always feel the power of their teacher, the unique mastery of being where they most expect you to be, fully alive, vital, without doubt—and then like magic, somewhere else unexpectedly. A shadow of illusion. Deception, stealth, and formidable threats throw the students in a mass of confusion as the teacher tactically unfolds his state of absolute reign and mastery. Even with all the ability, the teacher maintains some decorum and ultimate control in and out of battle, always aware not to damage those whom he is charged to cultivate in body and mind. The hidden powers and ever-present unchained spirit are held in reserve for the appropriate time and in this fight the moment grew close. Aloof and razor-sharp, the teacher knows when to cut off the head of the spike.

With the boldness of honor and the abandonment of apathy, I shouted, *"Ikimassho!"* The wall was slippery from the sweat of bodies slamming against it. My opponent became frustrated, and as expected, used the brawn of his head versus the subtleties of the mind to advance. This was the New South Wales boys' last stop before catching the plane heading back for home—and this was to be my opponent's final leg of the battle journey he had so overconfidently underestimated. He would arrive home filled with excuses for his failure. I would make sure of this. I had a firm resolve to send these men home in a disenchanted frame of mind. They would have a lesson in *Budo*.

The time had come.

I thought back to the *dojo* in which I came to understand battle— *jigoku* (hell) *dojo,* as it was called in the olden days. The facade of deadly determination became apparent. I had to set a precedent at this school. My clenched fist became a hammer, a driving mallet destined to find its mark. I enticed him to come in, to advance his counterattack and commit. He dodged and slammed a kick into my thigh. A stinging sensation ran up my leg. Once again, I slipped his attack, ducked a hook, and covered from an upper cut. I dropped my elbow to meet his punch. Smash! I felt him connect, and to my pleasure his hand disintegrated. Instantly, I countered with an elbow to the forehead. I connected and held back penetration in reserve. His eye opened up and blood began to flow. Instead of stopping, we both continued the engagement.

Again he attacked, but ducking inside to hook to my kidneys in a barrage. I moved out of range, snuck back inside, and wrapped one arm around his head and trapped his other arm. Pushing, then pulling, I snapped my hip over for a throw and over he came. Shifting my leg across and outside his legs I swept upward, breaking his balance and sending his lower body high into the air as he flew over me. Down on the *tatami* he came. Unfortunately, he held on to my side (instinctively a response for someone who hasn't trained in throws) instead of breaking his fall, which I took advantage of by following him down. What he didn't understand was that my weight would now fall on top of him full force, compounding the throw. Bad move on his part.

As we collided with the floor, my rib cage slammed into his, and my shoulder rolled over his jaw. I knew this was of vital importance to winning in combat during a throw. If you hang for the ride you suffer the consequences. Richard stood back up, one of his eyes swollen almost shut, the facial skin across his jaw burned from my uniform as my shoulder ripped through on the fall. Blood still flowed from his other lacerated eye. He motioned for me to keep coming. I began to feel dissatisfied in my determined battle. I had won long ago but was faced with the decision to stop his advance altogether. He came rushing again with jabs and upper cuts. I engaged in grappling and began to smother his attack in preparation for another sweep and throw.

A couple of interested spectators who had inquired earlier about lessons looked on, but only briefly before making a hasty exit in witness to the brutal engagement. I knew they would not be back for a second look. Most newcomers, let alone dedicated students, rarely see their *sensei* in action, especially in this manner. What a student dreamed of seeing became a reality this evening.

Tying up, I let loose an explosive display of true *karate-do* in action. I hung on and let elbows fly to the head, my knees thrust into his midsection, allowing my energy to let loose everything I had short of total destruction. I felt my elbow contact the cerebrum, and I heard the gust of wind exit his body as the knee and shin-swinging roundhouse style wreaked havoc on his upper ribs. Richard the kickboxer was reincarnated, reborn into the world of truthful martial arts. My shins were hardened from years of relentless sandbag training, and my elbows were like mallets from *makiwara*. I knew the capable arsenal at my disposal, and so did those in the *dojo*. I left my mark that summer night to be carried to a distant land, and a lesson for all to remember. One's actions are of total importance, as they remain with one over the years. As you come to understand the self, you come to live with the memories of days long gone. These were his stories, these were the grueling days of combat a *bujin* lives to recall as the hair turns grey and the heart grows compassionate through time. We carry ourselves wherever we go; be it guilt or honor, it remains.

The traditional *bujin* was conditioned on every level of hierarchy. He was required to treat his superiors in a highly deferential manner, to anticipate and fulfill their every whim—all with precisely prescribed etiquette *(saho)*. Training became the mainstay, along with the most difficult realization—"To Just Do." A true *bujin* learned to meticulously practice not only battle but to serve as a role model for others. Etiquette became the ritual in martial arts society, and enforcement of prevailing ethics was harsh and swift. Etiquette took precedence over principle. The ritual of the *dojo*, the loyal service to a cause, and the code of rectitude (uprightness)—that of serving by martial representation—was all-inclusive.

In one final charge, I grabbed Richard's belt, trapped his left shoulder under my arm and, squeezing tight, lifted, twisted, and swept both feet from under him and dropped him full power on the *tatami*. Lying there, he looked up at me disillusioned, dumbfounded, and conquered. The impact seemed to create confusion in his mind.

I bent down and looked over him from toe to head, then held my gaze on his eyes and quietly spoke, "Enough." He was truly a soldier of heart, a battle-oriented warrior who loved the art of contact in its purest form. I knew his spirit was bruised, but he would come back at another time, another *dojo,* perhaps even more worthy of his new-found realization. This event was a lesson to his ego, a shot in the heart and an open door to new horizons of knowledge lest he give up. No, he would continue to learn and die a thousand times with earth, wind, and fire.

His eyes glazed over. I stood up quickly and he clumsily attempted to follow as best he could in his state. We both faced one another, bowed, and regained rational senses. I was as fresh as newborn spring, strong as the driving sea, and calm as a pine forest. I experienced *satori*. It lingered on and off for moments at a time, a reflection of serenity while in the jaws of conflict. Even more fulfilling was my magnificent private *zanshin*. I wanted to fight more, to continue on. But no one was left. The basis for any engagement was perfect focus at the edge of time.

> "A place where armor clashed against armor and swords
> ripped and tore into flesh. The battle forces of
> both mind and spirit stood poised for a moment, then
> charged into the pit of warfare as skill and fate
> proved success or death in an instant. Perhaps
> this was what enlightenment was or is."

I motioned all those present to begin *soji* (*dojo* cleanup). As various students manned brooms and cleaning material for the ritual of cleaning the *tatami* equipment, I walked up front to enter my office. Closing the doors for privacy, I grabbed my thigh, which had been damaged from a collision with Richard's knee or a sweep he used that

I had forgotten in the heat of battle. During *kumite* one becomes impenetrable to a host of different injuries when the mind is focused on winning and surviving. I knew that I would not be able to walk, as the evening wore on. The muscle would tighten up to a point of cramping, and my only friend would be an ice pack and time to heal. Homeward I would go, so my love could help me recover.

Quickly, I temporarily wrapped my leg so as not to express defeat in any manner, and made my way toward the locker room, where all the warriors gathered for cold beer and discussions with each other on their battles. I was stopped by several juniors on the way for information regarding *kumite*. I answered quickly as I walked and finally arrived at the locker room entrance.

The locker room was crowded by warriors who tended their injuries and drank while preparing for their departure. A few of the advanced men would share their views with our guests or, I should say, victims. I turned to my right to see the vanquished changing up. I asked Donald if he enjoyed himself and he simply answered, "I've got to get out of here, my foot is killing me." I glanced over to Richard to find his face swollen and bloody. Both eyes were partially shut and he would need stitches for several cuts. I asked one of my students to take them to the med center if they required medical care.

"Richard," I asked, "What do you think of this training method we use against the wall?"

"I really can't give you a logical answer right now, but this is certainly our last and final stop on our tour," he responded.

Sarcastically I commented, "At least you can return to your *dojo* with a few good stories about the U.S.A. and our style. By the way, you both did fairly well tonight. I hope you can return some day." The kickboxers had little more to say.

We exchanged addresses and telephone numbers for future reference and escorted them to the front door. I never did hear from them again. Don walked with an exaggerated limp as he carried his training gear under his right arm. Richard, the best of the two in spirit and heart, was entirely a mess. Holding his training gear under his right arm, he slowly made his way to the *genkan*. He walked with a tilt and his left arm pressed against his left side, held there as if to relieve the pressure from the broken or fractured ribs beneath the surface. We offered twice to take them to the med center for an exam of injuries, but ego or pride drew up internal anger and perhaps honor. Our assistance was refused. I knew their flight tomorrow would last some ten or twelve hours back to New South Wales and in all would be an uncomfortable journey. Defeat can be an eye opener or, in Richard's case, an eye closer.

In retrospect, I learned a great deal about myself. Never underestimate your opponent, be it his size, manner, or his words. Much training was before me and a new journey had started once again.

The opponent must be stopped immediately. The longer the battle, the greater the threat of personal casualty. Vulnerability must be found in the opponent quickly, and tactics need to be resolved without haste. One must be swift in stratagems, consider battle plans, and above all, never become overconfident in mind or body. It became evident that in the heat of actual battle, cheap talk may be a start but was no alternative to results. Action breeds the heroes who carry the torch to victory. We create our own history, shape our own destiny, and learn from the history of others.

> A real leader displays his quality in his triumphs over adversity, however great it may be.
> —General G. C. Marshall, Fort Benning, Georgia

Time was growing short. I had to get home, rest, and prepare for practice in the morning. I lived for it.